Operation
Sea Angler

Operation
SEA ANGLER

Mike Ladle

WITH

Harry Casey & Terry Gledhill

Adam & Charles Black · London

First published 1983

A & C Black (Publishers) Limited
35 Bedford Row, London WC1R 4JH

Ladle, Mike
    Operation sea angler.
    1. Saltwater fishing
    I. Title   II. Casey, Harry
    III. Gledhill, Terry
    799.1'6   SH457

    ISBN 0-7136-2369-1

ISBN 0-7136-2369-1

Printed and bound in Great Britain by R. J. Acford, Chichester, Sussex

Contents

List of illustrations

PHOTOGRAPHS

LINE DRAWINGS

The text includes 49 explanatory line drawings

Introduction

Three anglers stood up to their knees in a sticky, smelly, decaying mountain of seaweed. Their casting arms were working overtime, not that they had to cast very far. Before them the surface of the sea heaved and boiled with feeding mullet ranging in size from that of a herring to near record proportions.

The fish were ravenously scooping in maggots from the creamy scum which laced the surface of the water. Back and forth they cruised, twisting and turning as they searched for the greatest concentration of food.

The rod of one angler bent double and the ratchet screamed as thirty yards of line were torn off in a few seconds. His plimsoll-clad feet stumbled over the hummocks of decaying wrack and the breaking waves surged up his bare legs as, rod held high, he followed the course of the hooked fish along the beach. Fragments of weed flew in all directions as the fish again sped out to sea. In the ensuing battle, angler and fish alternately gained control, but gradually, under the relentless pressure, the mullet began to tire. Five minutes later a 4-pound mullet was drawn over the rim of the large net held by one of the other anglers.

As they turned to face the sea, their companion was into another good fish. One of them, net in hand, hurried along to lend assistance, the other picked up his rod and again began to cast to a group of milling fish. Hardly had the second mullet been landed before the last of the trio struck firmly. His rod flexed and line streamed from the reel. The fish slowed briefly and boiled on the surface twenty yards out, revealing as it did so the tell-tale prickly dorsal-fin of a large bass, before accelerating into a second run. The light glass rod curved ever more steeply as the knot joining fly-line to backing jammed on the second ring. Inevitably the cast parted and the line fell slack.

Sport continued unabated for the next hour before the tide turned and the increasing surf dispersed the mullet shoals.

The red sun of the summer evening was merging with the top of the western cliffs as the three gathered up their tackle and compared their respective catches. The first carried four mullet of 3-4 pounds each, the second had three similar mullet and a fine $5\frac{1}{2}$-pound bass. A broad smile on the face of the third angler hinted that his catch was something special. Side by side on the dark grey shale by his feet lay five mullet with a total weight of over 25-pounds.

As they trudged slowly back along the shore in the gathering gloom they thought and talked of those early days when they had first arrived in Dorset.

ACKNOWLEDGEMENTS

We wish to thank the Council of the Freshwater Biological Association for allowing us to publish this book and all the anglers who have helped us to make it possible. In particular our thanks are due to Trevor Crisp for passing on some of his own interesting observations.

Mike Ladle
Harry Casey
Terence Gledhill

1

'You should have been here last week!'

THE HOW, WHERE, WHEN and WHY

In the mid-1960s coincidence brought together in Dorset a group of enthusiastic anglers from various parts of the country. Their angling experience ranged from fly-fishing in the picturesque rivers, lakes and tarns of Cumbria to handlining for coalfish and flounders from the greystone jetties of Northumbrian fishing villages and fishing for roach and perch in the less picturesque ponds and canals around Liverpool.

Harry, Terry and myself - a Scouser and two Yorkshiremen - were the mainstay of the group. Since that time the number of fanatics involved has fluctuated over the years but the originators fish on to the present day despite the demands of wives, children, mortgages, violent sport, and even the dreaded gardens and allotments. Because of these commitments, fishing time is and always has been at a premium, so it was continually necessary to try and obtain the best return for our efforts (hopefully the best chance of catching fish). The same must apply to many other anglers although a fair proportion of writers seem to regard the catch as a surprise bonus. Necessity is the mother of invention and this book relates how we have streamlined and modified our approaches to sea fishing. By careful consideration of the habits of fish and their food, by observation, by experiment, by hard work and, above all, by persistent application of methods appropriate to the fish and the sea conditions, we have managed to improve our catches.

At first we fished in a more or less random manner over most of the coastline from Bournemouth to Chesil Beach. We used traditional sea fishing rods, tackles and baits. At least twice a week, throughout the year, rain, hail or shine, we made our pilgrimage to the sea. From the angling weeklies, glossy magazines and books we absorbed every scrap of information

1

about the local angling *hotspots* and the fine fish being caught in our area.

During the summer months we fished in daylight from Poole Quay. Sitting on the quayside, under the feet of strolling holidaymakers and float fishing or legering between the ropes of the moored yachts and freighters, we caught small bass, wrasse, flounders, gobies, sand smelts and mullet. In the dark winter evenings, clothed in murk and drizzle, after the holidaymakers had gone, we added rocklings, small pouting and poor cod.

The steep shingle slopes of the famous Chesil Beach provided wrasse, mackerel, pollack, small bass, flatfish, whiting, eels and bullheads. From other beaches, cliffs and ledges in between, the results were much the same with only the proportions of the various species changing. A good fish meant a red–letter day.

Clearly, summer and winter, day and night, a considerable variety of fish were feeding close inshore but we were mostly catching only the smaller and more gullible specimens. It was a difficult pill to swallow, but it was painfully obvious that we knew little of the nature and habits of the fish we sought. A decision was made to set about collecting hard facts, rather than hearsay, on the food and feeding, migrations and behaviour of sea fishes. The object was to improve our catches in terms of regularity, numbers and size of fish and to fish selectively for particular species.

All the experts, local and national, had their own favourite hypotheses as to *how* fish could be caught. Most of these were found wanting for lack of information on *where* and *when* and all were generally unconvincing because they left the question *why* unanswered, apart from vague speculation. Only rarely were theories backed up by detailed accounts of the resultant catches.

The question of what to fish for was clearly an important one. Firstly it was dictated by the species which were known to occur along local shores. Secondly it was a matter of which of these appealed to us most, an appeal which has changed over the years as the major problems posed by each were more or less solved.

Having decided what we wished to catch, four main factors had to be considered, these being the ones on which we would base our approach.

Firstly, where should we fish? Details were to be found either in published articles, by asking local anglers or, more reliably, by watching other people fish, and by our own trial and error. Shores in different parts of Britain are inhabited by characteristic and different species of fish and within each region certain spots have acquired, sometimes deservedly, reputations as good places for particular fish. Much of our local coastline appeared rarely to be fished and still less to be mentioned in the press. Information was only to be had by trying it out.

Secondly, there was the time of year and time of day to be considered. Broadly, it seemed sufficient to look at the year in terms of twelve months and the day as being divided into four periods — daylight, darkness, dawn and dusk. In shallow waters pouting and conger are recognised as mainly nocturnal, whereas wrasse and mackerel are usually caught during the hours of daylight. Dusk is often quoted as a key time, particularly for pollack. In most cases it is uncertain to what extent these impressions are due to the habits of anglers and how much they result from the behaviour of the fish in question. Exceptions to the rules are commonplace.

The third factor to consider was the state of the tide. Springs or neaps, ebb or flood, high or low water—which is best? The frequently quoted advice is to find the best state of the tide for each fishing place. Rarely is this advice accompanied by the essential bit of information on how to do this; presumably the tedious process of trial and error is implied.

Finally, the weather is of great importance. Bearing in mind the obvious point that some exposed beaches and rocks are not only unfishable, but down-right dangerous in rough weather; and also the much quoted liking of bass for a *good surf*, very little attention is normally paid to weather conditions.

In short, what are the right places and the right times? If we knew *all* the answers we would be out fishing instead of writing a book; at this moment, on some beach, the conditions are perfect for making a good catch. There are so many possible permutations of place, time, tide and weather that for an angler to find the correct combination every time would make solving Rubik's Cube seem like light entertainment for chimpanzees. However, by a reasonably systematic approach, by noting recurrent patterns of events and, above all, by many hours of observing and fishing, it has been possible to develop methods in which we, at least, have confidence. Of course we don't catch good fish every time we go fishing, but then—who does?

Subject to the vagaries of the climate of the British Isles the seasons of the year come round with pleasing regularity. Associated with these seasons are the annual breeding and feeding migrations of various species of sea fish. Among the best known of these is the spring dispersion of huge shoals of mackerel from the Continental shelf off south-west England and from the regions offshore of southern Norway. In November and December the fish are massed on the sea bed and feed little, taking only small numbers of crustaceans, worms and small fish. From December to

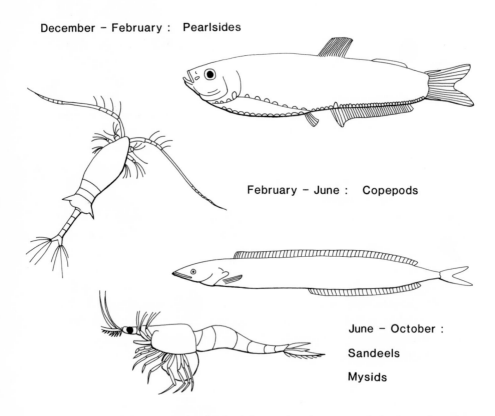

December – February :   Pearlsides

February – June :   Copepods

June – October :

Sandeels

Mysids

1. Seasonal changes in the food of the mackerel. Not much feeding takes place in November and December.

February the mackerel move in towards the coast and, during this period, migrate towards the surface of the sea during the hours of darkness, gradually forming surface shoals. In this phase of their migration the mackerel eat small fish such as the tiny silver pearlside, only an inch or two in length and having a belly lined with pale-blue luminous dots. In late winter and spring the fish move into their spawning areas before spreading out around our coast. During this shoaling phase the mackerel feed mainly on copepods, little drifting crustaceans about the size of rice grains.

Good commercial catches of mackerel are often taken in what fishermen term *yellow water*, rich in copepods. Poor catches are associated with greyish water having an unpleasant smell. In the June to October period the fish range along the coastline and the diet changes to small fish such as sand eels, together with some shrimps and prawns, before they return to the overwintering areas offshore. Along the coast of Cornwall, winter mackerel are caught on trolled feathers.

A second example of seasonal migration is seen in the cod which, in British waters, spawns in late winter and spring when water temperatures are about 4-6°C, one of the main spawning areas being in the eastern end of the English Channel. After spawning, the shoals of cod disperse to the feeding areas. Congregation for spawning seems to be the only systematic seasonal movement of these fish.

Examples such as these could be continued indefinitely, but knowledge of migrations is only of value to most anglers if the movements result in the fish coming comparatively close inshore. For much of the time large concentrations of spawning fish, whether they be mackerel, cod or other species, are far beyond the reach of beach or small-boat anglers. In a few cases, such as that of the black bream, an understanding of the spawning migration and habits is essential to angling success. In other cases the information is of only academic interest.

Superimposed on these spawning/feeding migrations are the activity patterns of each species. For example, the responses of fish to water temperatures. Those fishes which are near the northern limits of their distributions, such as conger and bass, tend to be more active in the warm months of the year. In contrast, cod and haddock are caught chiefly in winter and are mainly distributed to

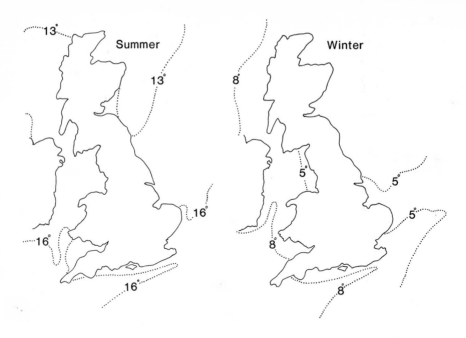

2. Summer and winter sea-surface temperatures around Britain. Cod prefer sea temperatures below 10°C.

the north of Britain. The main geographical area occupied by the cod lies between water temperatures of 0°C and 10°C and the annual mean isotherm for 10°C almost cuts the British Isles in two. Within the area which we fish, the sea surface temperature at Swanage reaches its minimum of about 7°C in February and for most of the year is well above 10°C. Most fish feed actively when the water temperature is well within the range for the area in which they normally live, i.e. neither too warm nor too cold.

Apart from the direct effects of water temperature, day–length etc. on the fish themselves, there are also the indirect influences of these factors on the food supply. In a normal year the spring months and lengthening days herald the development of a massive growth of microscopic drifting algae, itself stimulating an outburst of small planktonic animals. This zooplankton is soon supplemented by the numerous drifting larvae of bottom-living worms, crabs and clams and also the innumerable fry and young stages of the fish themselves. All of these tiny, vulnerable creatures provide food for larger fish.

On a daily basis, the twenty-four hour cycle of daylight and darkness is the trigger for rhythmic activity of many small animals. The best known of these patterns is the *vertical migration of the plankton*. This involves the active upward swimming of crustaceans and other forms at the approach of darkness, followed by the reverse movement in daytime. Although the creatures which make these migrations are small, the depths which they cover are surprisingly great, commonly ranging from as much as twenty fathoms (120 feet) deep at noon, up to the surface at dusk and returning again to the same depth just before dawn.

Obviously it is an advantage to fish such as mackerel, horse mackerel, garfish or herring, which feed on these creatures, to make similar migrations to those of their prey. This is precisely what they do. Herrings form shoals on the sea bed in the daylight hours and swim almost at the surface of the sea at night. However, when the water is turbid due to storm disturbance or dense plankton growth the fish will also spend the hours of daylight nearer the surface.

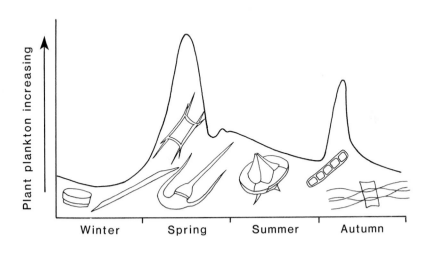

3.   Seasonal variations in the amount of plant plankton in the sea. These tiny plants are eaten by many fish-food animals and are most abundant in the spring.

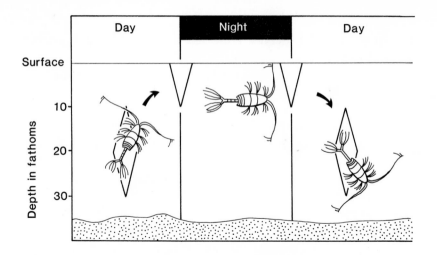

4. Vertical migration of Calanus. Although they are only the size of rice grains, these tiny animals swim to the surface at dawn and dusk and descend to 20 fathoms in the daytime.

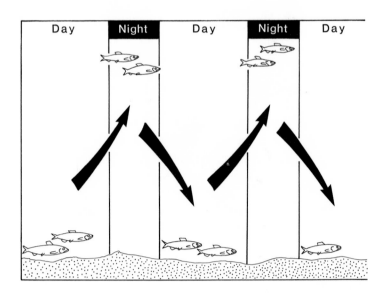

5. Daily pattern of vertical migration in the herring. Other surface-swimming fishes show similar patterns.

Larger predatory fish also swim towards the surface at night to feed on mackerel, horse mackerel and the like. Hake, for example, are near the sea bed in deep water during the daytime but feed *almost exclusively* in mid-water in the hours of darkness.

Of more obvious importance to the shore angler is the curious behaviour of the night-tidal plankton. Every sandy beach is inhabited by a great variety of clams, worms and beach hoppers which, at all states of the tide, spend the daylight hours well hidden in their burrows. They are normally only to be seen by washing a spadeful of sand through a fine sieve. At night the beach hoppers in particular, emerge from their hiding places to swim actively in the surf. At this time they become available to foraging pouting, school bass and dabs. One of the main reasons for this behaviour is the dispersal of male beach hoppers in their search for mates. In consequence there is a much higher proportion of males in the surf than burrowing in the beach. The number of these animals in the surf is greatest in July and there are other peaks in April and September. Most are swimming just after dusk and before dawn. Rough conditions also cause an increase in the amounts of activity, but most still occur after dark.

A daily cycle of activity is also shown by the common brown shrimp which lives on sandy beaches. Normally, when the tide is out, these shrimps burrow in the sand below the low water mark. As the tide rises the shrimps leave the sand and disperse by swimming in the water. Bright light partly prevents swimming behaviour so that most activity occurs on flood tides in the hours of darkness or, notably, when rough seas colour the water.

All this nocturnal activity, often centred on two periods round about dusk and just before dawn, is closely associated with the feeding habits of small fish such as pouting, rocklings, poor cod, gobies and sole. In our area pouting and poor cod are often so numerous that fishing for other species after dark, with small baits, is scarcely worthwhile.

These are just a few examples of what is behind the success of angling at particular times of the day or year. Additional cases related to commonly used baits will be given in the following chapters. Too many variations occur for all the possibilities to be dealt with but the angler should be able to work out the best approach for the fish of his or her choice.

A peculiar phenomenon rather different to the above, is the so-called *selective tidal stream transport* behaviour of fish. This occurs in some species which are of interest to the angler. Enquiries among Dutch commercial fishermen revealed that in spring, prior to spawning, the common sole swims up to the surface of the sea. This takes place at night when the tidal currents are flowing towards the coast. When they reach the surface, the fish lie immobile and adopt a posture which presents a large surface area to the water currents. In this way they are able to drift, with a minimum of effort, from deep water feeding grounds towards inshore spawning areas. There is some evidence that the fish may navigate by the stars.

A similar form of behaviour has been noted in the plaice and it would seem likely that other fishes use the same means of transport. While night fishing from a small rowing dinghy on calm nights in late summer, the authors have observed, in the light of a torch, small groups of three or four garfish drifting passively with the ebb current, a foot or two below the water

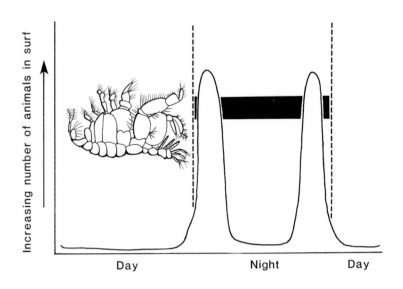

6. Dawn and dusk pattern of swimming in the surf by the so-called 'Night-tidal plankton'. These animals spend the daylight hours burrowing in the beach sand.

surface. Possibly this is an example of a similar energy conservation measure. In any event it is a tiny but fascinating piece of the piscatorial jigsaw puzzle.

In the following chapters it will be clear that most of our fishing is done from rock and shingle beaches or from small rowing dinghies. We have little experience of grip-leads and 200-yard casts, of cliff climbing methods and heavy tackle used by anglers here or in other parts of the country, or of flying collars and thousand-pound catches of pollack and ling from wrecks. This is not because we have any aversion to these methods, but because we feel that success only comes by specialisation and our eggs are already distributed across a wide range of baskets.

We read of, and discuss with awe, some of the catches of other anglers; our hope is that the ideas and approaches described in these pages may provide food for thought for the beginner and expert alike, whatever their pleasure. Perhaps it is not too presumptuous to suppose that someone may catch a few more fish after reading of our failures and successes.

2

Food, glorious food!

WHAT FISH EAT

Returning to the subject of food, it is well worth looking at the yearly cycles of some of the most important bait/food organisms and trying to establish when they are most likely to be available to the fish which eat them.

Firstly there is the ubiquitous lugworm. These plump worms are widely used as bait, probably because they make a good hookful of material which is acceptable to a wide range of fishes. Also, they are comparatively easy to find and dig from shores of sand and muddy sand. Lugworms occur both on the open coast and in sheltered bays and estuaries; the so-called black lug, gullies, and so-forth, are varieties of the same species and differ because of local conditions. A very similar species, the tailless lugworm, is found on stony or gravelly ground. Fish which feed on these worms are thus accustomed to finding one or other species in most intertidal areas.

The common lugworm, whose little spirals of sand are such a conspicuous feature of our beaches, is normally well protected in the U-shaped feeding burrow, where it lies pumping water down through the little sand-filter which provides its food and, at intervals, backs up to the surface to add to its cast. Only rarely can any portion of the worm's body protrude from its burrow and then only the expendable tip of its 'tail'.

Lugworm do, however, leave their burrows and would seem to be particularly vulnerable to fish twice a year. In particular, many worms may come to the surface at their spawning time. The lugworm releases eggs and sperm from within the safety of its burrow between spring tides in late October. At this time deaths following spawning can reduce the number of lugworm on a beach by as much as 40 per cent. and, for a short time, many dead worms may be found on the surface of the sand. Lugworm

12

also migrate by a form of swimming, which takes place at times not associated with spawning. Swimming worms have been seen in May, when bare stretches of beach may be quickly re-colonised. It seems probable that fish are especially attracted to lugworm beds, both below and between the tide marks, in May and in October-November. At these times they may even be conditioned to, or preoccupied with, feeding on these worms.

The king ragworm, another good big hookful and a very popular bait, has been studied on the aptly named Black Middens, a large area of mudflats near the mouth of the River Tyne in Northumberland (now Tyne and Wear). The most striking feature of these and other ragworms are the jaws which pop out and pinch the angler's finger as he baits up. They are not, as might be supposed, used for capturing the tiny algae and bits of

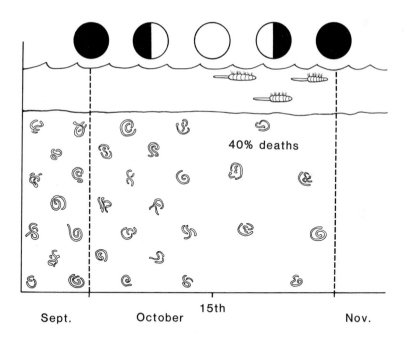

7.   Spawning of the lugworm. The worms spawn after the mid-October new moon. Spent 'dead' worms can be found on the surface of the sand after spawning.

detritus on which the worms feed. In fact, the pincers are weapons which are often employed to repel other ragworms from the burrow. The manner in which these jaws are used can be clearly seen if two worms are introduced at opposite ends of a piece of glass tube immersed in a dish of sea water. The king rag lives on mudflats, often close to and under large stones. Several other species of ragworm are used for bait, notably the small red harbour ragworm which lives on the upper levels of the shore. These red ragworms are always most abundant where freshwater runs over or percolates through the sediment.

King ragworms are dug for use and for sale as bait. The extent to which bait diggers remove large worms on the Black Middens is as high as 75-80 per cent. It takes about a month for a dug out patch to repopulate from surrounding areas. Spawning of king rag takes place in May and large numbers of tiny worms appear on the flats in July and August, having either grown and developed on the shore or migrated from below the tide marks. The worms then live and grow in the mud for two or three years.

Female worms remain in their winding burrows to spawn, releasing their eggs into the overlying water. In contrast the male worms turn deep green, develop extra large swimming paddles at spawning time and release their sperm while swarming in the

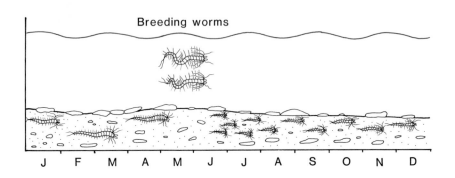

8.   Spawning of the king-ragworm. Male worms leave the burrows to spawn in May. Females release eggs from within burrows.

water above the burrows. At this time (in late spring) they will be readily caught and eaten by fish. The male worms swim in a curious manner with the front part of the body held out stiffly and the back end wriggling, rather like some of the modern, soft plastic, 'sand eel' lures. Some anglers will not use green breeding ragworms for bait because they are thought not to be attractive to fish. We cannot comment on this statement but would be interested in any evidence that breeding worms are distasteful to fish.

Molluscs such as mussels, cockles and clams, are widely used as bait. In the north of England the mussel is the favourite. Easily available to the angler in large quantities these bivalves inhabit exposed rocky shores and stony, muddy estuaries. Mussels are usually firmly attached and well protected from fish predators, with the possible exception of wrasse, which have very powerful teeth. Mussels are attacked and eaten, however, notably by starfish, shore crabs, edible crabs and oyster catchers, all of which must leave remains to be eaten by fish. They are rightly regarded as a good bait, for cod and flatfish in particular. Probably because they have to be shelled and are a little difficult to hook they are not much used by anglers in our area.

Here in the south, the slipper limpet, an alien snail introduced by man from the west Atlantic, provides an alternative bait to mussel. Slipper limpets are easy to extract from their shells and are a good deal tougher than mussels, but they are, in our experience, not quite so attractive to most fish. These limpets occur in masses with the smaller specimens on top of the pile. Large limpets are all females, having begun their lives as small males and changed sex as they aged.

Crab is regarded by many anglers throughout the country as the premier bait for a wide variety of the more popular fish species. Green shore crabs are usually the easiest to obtain and enormous numbers of these can be collected in a short time from harbours, estuaries and rocky shores. The ordinary hard-crab is useful as groundbait and makes a first class hookbait for large wrasse but, despite much speculation to the contrary, no-one has ever presented evidence of catches to show that they are a good general bait. Usually, crabs of all types are collected and used as bait when they are about to moult (peelers) or have just moulted (soft-backs). Crabs grow and moult most frequently when they are young and in warm weather. A convenient way of recognising both peeler and soft-back crabs is to look for pairs. The males can infallibly detect females which are about to shed their shells and carry them about until they moult, at which time mating occurs. On the west coast this mostly is in August and September. The females do not produce their eggs until the following April-May, though in our part of the country they are also found in winter. Other than pairs, peeler and soft-crabs of the three common species can be found at almost any time of year, but will be most frequent in the warmer months.

Other crustaceans eaten by fish and used as bait by anglers are shrimps and prawns. The daily tidal rhythm of the brown shrimp which lives on sandy beaches has already been mentioned. The

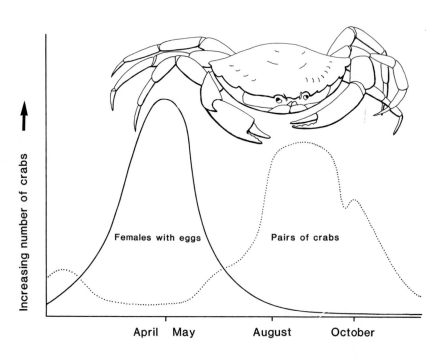

9. Breeding of the shore-crab. Crabs moult most frequently in the warmer months but pairs of crabs (with peeling or soft females) are found in late summer. Eggs are mostly laid in April-May.

equivalents of these animals on rocky and weedy shores are several species of prawn. These are all used as bait, particularly in the south and west of the country where fish such as bass, wrasse and pollack take them readily. The two common species of prawns are to be found in rock pools throughout the summer months. The larger of the two (up to three inches in length) migrates offshore in winter and is normally found at lower tidal levels than its smaller counterpart, even in summer. Both of these prawns become very active on the ebb of the spring tides and they also exhibit dusk and dawn periods of swimming during the neaps.

An interesting aspect of prawn behaviour, in relation to the feeding of bass, was related to us by the late Bert Randall of Weymouth. In the course of his life Bert must have spent as many hours watching fish, catching fish and watching other people catch fish as anyone in the country. In his youth he used to tend the small-mesh pots used in this part of the country to catch prawns. Often he would drop a large prawn into the deep clear water where he could see bass swimming. The prawn would sink slowly with its body held stiff and straight and its spear-like rostrum projecting in front. In this state the prawn was rarely attacked by a bass, but as it approached the sea bed it would usually flex its tail and dart for cover. At this instant the bass would react and make its lunge in an attempt to capture its prey. Presumably the fish respond to a combination of form and movement in the way that is often referred to by wet-fly fishermen. Bait presentation can obviously be very important in sea fishing.

Because they are easily obtainable in large quantities from fishmongers and tackle shops, squid and cuttlefish are popular baits. The squids sold are mostly those imported from the Pacific Ocean and, in their dead, frozen state they are pinkish, leathery and rather tough. Less commonly appreciated is the great abundance and variety of squids and cuttlefishes which swim in the seas around the British Isles. The living creatures are mostly fast-swimming, streamlined, opalescent, translucent animals. The species eaten by fishes include the tiny little-cuttles, several species of which are very abundant offshore, near the sea bed. One of these, *Sepiola,* is found in enormous numbers just below the low water mark off sandy beaches and is sometimes present in the guts of fish from such places.

The larger common cuttlefish is active at night and may be over one foot in length. Its internal shell or cuttlebone is often cast up with the flotsam and jetsam along the tideline. Cuttlefish live on sandy sea beds, feeding after dark on shrimps which they disturb by projecting jets of water onto the sand and seize by using the two longest tentacles. The cuttlebone is used rather like the ballast tank of a submarine. By varying the amount of fluid in the bone the cuttlefish can control its buoyancy and is able to swim either slowly by rippling the marginal fin or quickly by jet propulsion. These molluscs live for about three years and very cold spells in winter may cause mass deaths. At these times thousands of dead cuttlefish and their bones may be washed up on beaches. Like squid and octopus, cuttlefish are masters of colour change. Although they are normally well camouflaged, cuttlefish blanch when they are scared and develop two enormous eye spots, a pattern which is presumably a last resort in trying to repel large fish. It also suggests that their predators are susceptible to such threats.

Squid generally live further from the sea bed than cuttlefish; they are even more streamlined and very active. The internal shell of squids is reduced to a sliver of plastic-like stiffening material. The large squid *Loligo forbesi* is common around Britain and may grow to two-and-a-half feet long. Occasionally we have caught these squids in winter when fishing at night for conger from our local beaches. Many of the abortive runs which occur when using fish baits from the shore and from boats may be due to the attentions of squid or cuttlefish. Squid feed on crustaceans, smaller squids and fish. These molluscs bite off the heads of fish in a characteristic manner and this may assist in the recognition of squid-bitten baits.

Large numbers of *Loligo* are netted some miles off the Yorkshire coast, but smaller species, rarely more than six inches in length, are even more numerous. The latter closely resemble the Californian squids used as bait and they are known to be particularly abundant over deep water in winter and spring.

A favourite bait in the south-west of England is the 'sand eel'. One of the most abundant species is Raitt's sand eel (*Ammodytes marinus*) a so-called *lesser* sand eel. P. Winslade used a photographic method to record the activity of these sand eels in tanks. In this way he was able to show that in summer, when the sea is richest in tiny, planktonic copepods which are the main food of the eels, the latter show a strong daily rhythm. They emerge from the sand, to swim and feed, only in the hours of daylight, burrowing back into the sand at dusk.

Quite a lot of light is required for the full daytime activity to develop. In more than a few fathoms of water in winter it is normally too gloomy for this to occur. The main feeding period of this sand eel is in April to July, after which, fat from their rich feeding, they tend to stay buried as their eggs mature prior to spawning in late winter. Spawning takes place later further north. The other common species of lesser sand eel (*A. tobianus*) has both spring and autumn spawning races. Fishes such as turbot, brill and blonde ray, which feed largely on sand eels, are mostly day-active and probably follow behaviour patterns similar to those of the sand eels.

Because all the food/bait organisms mentioned are very abundant but normally well able to take care of themselves, they

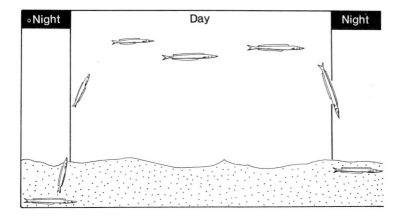

10.   Daily activity pattern of the lesser sand-eel. These 'eels' are day active when there is food (plankton) in the water and at dawn they poke their heads out of the sand.

are likely to be most successful as bait when injury, spawning or other migrations, storm disturbance or tidal movements make them easily available to fish. In effect, any large concentration of a particular food item is a sort of natural rubby dubby or groundbait. Often these concentrations are on a scale vastly greater than any which the angler could consider providing. To take advantage of such events they must be recognised or, preferably, anticipated. A classic example of such an event is the tidal rhythm of washout of the maggots of the seaweed fly.

The seaweed fly (*Coelopa frigida*) is one of five species of black, bristly flies which buzz about in clouds on the seashore to the consternation of holidaymakers. Their larvae, about the size of housefly maggots, live in the piles of rotting seaweed cast up near the high water mark of spring tides. These flies came into the news in 1953-4, when a veritable plague occurred on the coasts of southern England. The adult flies are irresistibly attracted to cleaning fluids. Factories where carbon tetrachloride or chloroform were used as solvents were inundated with the insects.

The flies normally breed throughout the year and occur on beaches from the English Channel to the Shetlands. Several other types of flies and a number of beetles are also found in rotting weed. Like most other insects, the seaweed fly goes through the stages of egg, larva, pupa and adult. The maggots and pupae have little breathing tubes at the back end. The life cycle takes about three weeks to complete with the maggots growing quickly in the heat generated by the decaying weed. The numbers of flies are governed chiefly by the quantity of rotting weed available as food. Adult flies normally stay in the weed unless they are disturbed by the rising tide, when they congregate and fly in swarms along the beach.

At the top of the spring tides the maggots of these flies are often washed into and onto the surface of the sea where, because they are lighter than the sea water, they float in masses, providing an irresistible attraction to fish such as sand smelts, mullet and bass.

This seaweed fly food source is not restricted to Britain. For example, vast amounts of kelp (between ten thousand and one million tons per year) are washed ashore on the beaches of California and act as a food source for flies and other insects in the

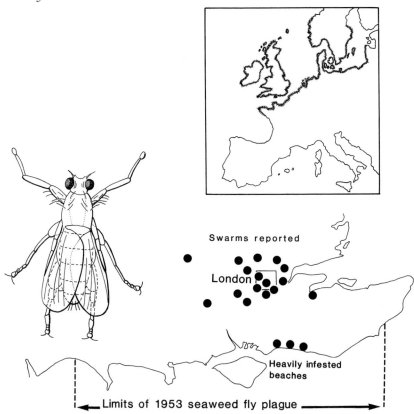

Swarms reported

London

Heavily infested
beaches

Limits of 1953 seaweed fly plague

11.   Distribution of the seaweed fly on the coasts of Europe and of the 1953
'plague' of flies on the south coast of England.

way already described. The number of flies is astronomical, with
up to twenty million on each mile of beach. These flies have a
ten-day life cycle in the summer months.

Other creatures which feed on weed and, in turn, attract and
are eaten by fish, include beach hoppers which live just above the
water line and isopods or marine woodlice just below it.

We have now discussed the activities and behaviour of some of
the most popular baits. If it is possible to match angling methods
and fishing times to such patterns, then catches should improve.
This has been the basis of our approach and, at least in some cases,
it has been successful.

3

'So what's the big attraction?'

WHY A FISH TAKES THE BAIT

Now we come to the tricky business of understanding the senses which fishes use to locate and identify their prey. The sense organs and degrees of awareness of fish have been described at length in many angling books but little attention has been paid to the much more relevant subject of fish feeding-behaviour. Experiments on the behaviour of fish or of any other group of animals, have to be carried out with exceptional care because it is only too easy to disturb the animals being studied. It is also possible inadvertently to teach or condition the fish to behave in an abnormal way.

A good example of experiments on fish feeding-behaviour was carried out with the marine, fifteen-spined stickleback. Although this is not an angler's fish in any sense, this study illustrated the importance of form and presentation of bait to any species. In this work the sticklebacks were given food in the form of mysids (opossum-shrimps), shrimp-like creatures of less than an inch in length with large prominent eyes and thin stick-like bodies. Each shrimp was fastened into a special tiny harness made from a slim glass tube, through which was threaded a loop of fine nylon line. The shrimps were then suspended on thin rods into a fish tank containing the sticklebacks. To avoid disturbance, the sticklebacks were observed through a narrow slit in a screen or by means of carefully arranged mirrors. Before each experiment each fish was starved for twenty-four hours and then released into the tank by the raising of a small trap door. Comparisons between still and moving prey were made by rotating the rods from which the shrimps were suspended by means of a little turntable operated by a variable speed motor.

The results of many experiments have been summarised in Table 1. It was shown that the most important factor in prey

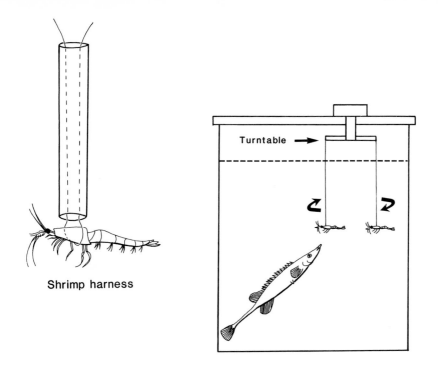

Shrimp harness

12. Experiment designed to show how the fifteen-spined stickleback selects its prey.

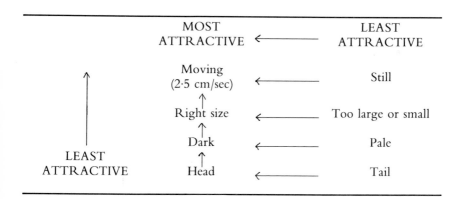

	MOST ATTRACTIVE ←	LEAST ATTRACTIVE
	Moving (2·5 cm/sec) ←	Still
	↑	
	Right size ←	Too large or small
	↑	
	Dark ←	Pale
LEAST ATTRACTIVE	↑	
	Head ←	Tail

TABLE 1 Prey selection by the fifteen-spined stickleback. Hungry fish are less fussy and the time which they need to 'handle' (deal with) prey is less.

selection was movement; a moving shrimp was almost always picked out in preference to a stationary one. Next in importance was size, the fish selecting shrimps of a preferred size rather than those which were either larger or smaller. Dark-coloured prey items were preferred to paler specimens. Lastly, the head ends of the prey induced much stronger feeding responses than did the tail ends, a preference which has also been demonstrated in larger predatory fish, such as the freshwater pike.

Clearly, in the case of the fifteen-spined stickleback at least, movement, size, colour and shape of the 'bait' are all-important. But there was also evidence that the effects of these features could be *additive*. In other words, the most attractive food would be of the correct size, shape and colour, moving in the right way at the preferred speed.

In another set of experiments it was shown that hungry fish were less fussy than well-fed fish, and that the 'handling time' of

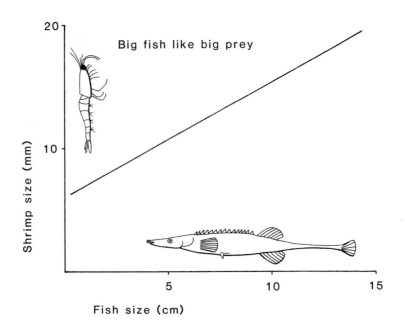

13.   The preferred prey sizes of the fifteen-spined stickleback.

prey was less in a hungry fish. This is just the sort of detail which could explain differences in the frequency and character of bites at different times. A nocturnal feeder such as the conger or pouting might thus be expected to give better bites in the evening at the start of the feeding period and *vice versa*.

When the fish were presented with a choice of prey size, it was clearly demonstrated, by examining stomach contents, that *large fish* preferred *large prey*. Similar big bait/big fish observations have been made on a number of other fishes and no doubt, in view of the experiences of many anglers, are widely applicable. This is not to say that large fish will not take small baits but that the more numerous small fish are liable to take small baits first.

A further species which has been the subject of investigation is the cod. Studies on the reactions of cod to objects and tastes (scents in the water) have been made. A series of tanks were used into which different particles or juices could be introduced to cod of between two inches and three feet in length.

Cod were shown to detect food in mid-water by sight and rarely missed any moving food. Even large cod could see tiny

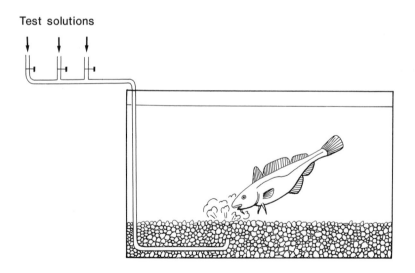

14. Experiment to show how the cod distinguishes food scents.

particles of food as small as one millimetre diameter, but four millimetres was about the smallest size to be taken consistently (nine times out of ten). Large pieces of food, laying on the stones on the bottom of the tank, were also detected by sight but small pieces were found by 'taste'. The cod swam along near the bottom of the tank with its barbel and the tips of the long, thin pelvic fins brushing the sea bed. When any of these three antennae, all of which are well armed with taste buds, touched a piece of food, the cod backed up and swallowed it. The taste of many different sea weeds, invertebrates and fish could be detected. Food hidden beneath stones or gravel was also found by smell/ taste and was uncovered by digging, which involved the fish lifting away stones in its mouth or rolling them away. A group of fish would cooperate in digging to uncover food, though food buried under sand was not detected. The feeding behaviour of one fish attracted others to the area. This is a good indication that, as in the case of flounders, attractor spoons and flashers really are worthwhile in cod fishing.

It is of some interest that in very cold water of less than 2°C, cod are not able to open their mouths widely and this limits the size of food taken.

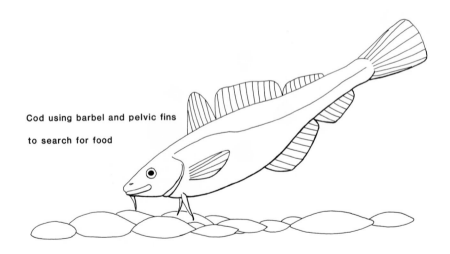

Cod using barbel and pelvic fins

to search for food

15.   The cod, using chin-barbel and pelvic fins as feelers to detect food lying on or under the 'sea-bed'.

Several members of the cod family have a triangle of sensory antennae like those of the cod itself. No doubt haddock, pouting and poor cod use their barbels and pelvic fins in a similar way to that described above.

Workers at the Fisheries Laboratory at Lowestoft examined the responses of cod to chemical attractants in water. They used a circular tank in which a current could be produced in either direction. An extract of squid in sea water was used as an attractant and the events recorded via a mirror through to a cine camera. In the absence of food or introduced squid extract the fish swam steadily downstream. The cod would pick up a piece of squid placed on the bottom of the tank but ignored the little pipe through which squid extract was to be introduced. Squid extract was trickled in upstream of and behind a fish which had just swum past the pipe. On its next circuit the fish sensed the extract, turned upstream and swam towards the pipe, searching from side to side and occasionally darting forwards. If it passed the pipe the fish turned and swam or drifted downstream until it again

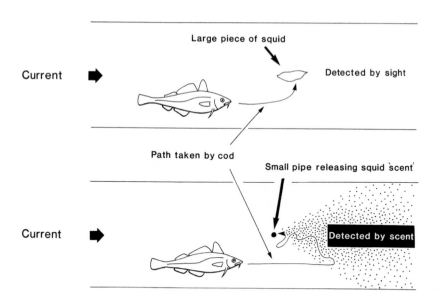

16. Experiment to show how the cod detects its food using both sight and 'smell'.

detected the scent. The mouth of the pipe was usually located in less than forty seconds.

Position of food	Sense used
Midwater	Sight (large items) Sight (movement) (small items)
Bottom	Sight (large items) Taste (small items)
Buried	Smell (found by digging, several fish may cooperate)

TABLE 2 Cod food detection

There is some evidence that other members of the cod family use a similar searching pattern in the sea, drifting with the tidal currents until the scent of food is detected and then turning upstream and following a scent trail. This method of search would be particularly important at night and in deep or dirty water.

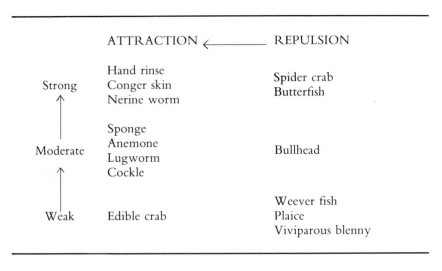

TABLE 3 Responses of cod to different 'odours'.

The cod was also the subject of experiments in which the degree of attraction to different dissolved odours was compared. To an angler the results are astonishing. The most attractive odours were those of conger eel skin, the nerine worm (a burrowing greenish worm with two long tentacles) and, thirdly, water used to rinse human hands. Extracts of spider crab and butter fish were the most strongly repulsive to the fish.

Perhaps at this stage examples of the food which has been found in both small and large cod should be presented. In general there is a change from foods such as shrimps, swimming crabs, porcelain crabs and butter fish (despite the fact that the scent of these fish was repulsive to the cod used in experiments) in the small fish, to Norway lobsters, sea mice and whiting in larger fish. All in all the cod is not a conservative feeder and clearly its feeding methods present considerable opportunities for experiment with both visual and scent/taste attractants.

Small cod	% CONTAINING FOOD Food item	Large cod
40	Shrimp	18
30	Swimming crab	
24	Porcelain crab	
16	Hermit crab	
16	Shore crab	
40 (Bullhead and Butterfish)	Fish	18 (whiting)
	Whelk	10
	Sea mouse	21
	Norway lobster	88

TABLE 4 Preferred foods of large and small cod.

The different members of the cod family take different foods. Fishes like haddock feed largely on brittle stars and hoppers, poor cod and pouting feed almost exclusively on crustaceans, and whiting and hake eat other fishes.

This family is also notable for the fact that some species

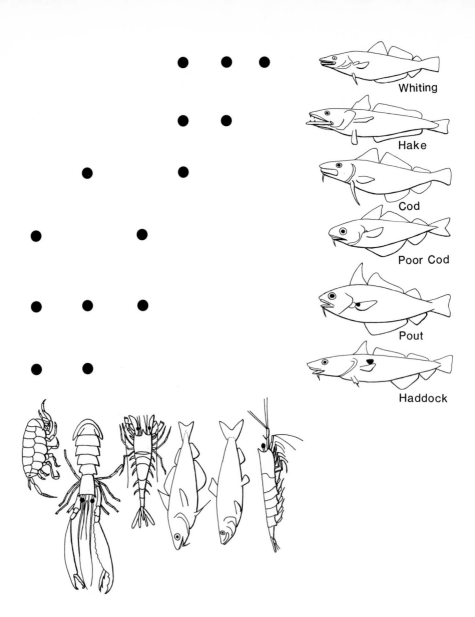

17. Food partitioning in some members of the cod family. Each species is adapted to certain main foods, ranging from the fish- and 'krill'-eating whiting to the hopper-eating haddock.

communicate vocally by means of grunts. Species which are not known to make sounds are whiting, coalfish, poor cod and three- and five-bearded rocklings. Vocal species include, apart from the cod itself, haddock, pollack and tadpole fish. The sounds are produced by vibrations of the swim bladder caused by muscles attached to it. The sounds are of low frequency and the rates of the sound pulses and their grouping differ from species to species. It would seem possible to devise audible means of attracting fish to the fishing area but the complexity of the subject suggests that it is probably not worthwhile.

4

Blow the wind Southerly

ON TIDES AND WEATHER

The tides, the weather, and the manner in which these affect the sea are crucial to understanding the behaviour and feeding patterns of sea fishes. The tides are due to a double bulge of water, on either side of the earth, caused by the attraction of the moon. If the moon was stationary in relation to the rotation of the earth, each coastal point on the earth's surface would experience high and low tides exactly twice in a twenty-four hour day. Because the moon is not fixed, the tides are later by about forty minutes each day. The obstruction of continents and land masses greatly alters the height and pattern of the tides.

Every two weeks, when the sun's attraction reinforces that of the moon, high water is exceptionally high and low water is exceptionally low; these are spring tides. Alternating with the spring tides are the neap tides which have a much smaller range. The biggest spring tides occur a couple of days after the full or the new moon, and on a particular stretch of coast they fall at approximately the same time of day. For example, on one of the beaches which we fish for bass, high water of the biggest spring tides is between 8 and 10 p.m. or just before dusk on a summer's evening.

As the earth rotates, the high water bulges (high tides) move from place to place; for instance, in the English Channel the high tide takes about six hours to advance from Plymouth to Dover. Due to the spin of the earth the channel water is flung towards the coast of France and so the tides are much higher (and lower) on the French coast than on the English coast.

The sequences of high and low waters, spring and neap tides are factors of vital importance in the lives of fishes. From the angler's point of view the indirect effects of the tidal rhythms are the most important because many of the creatures on which fish feed depend on the tides for timing their day-to-day lives. Between the tide marks, the breeding, feeding and migration activities of many worms, crabs, shrimps and prawns are often only possible when the tide is in. Even more striking is the way in which mass movements, which render the animals vulnerable to the fishes which eat them, take place only on tides of a certain height or even only on a few well defined tides each year. It is at these times that the bait organisms are most easily collected and most effective as bait.

The results of these tidal forces are profound and differ from one area to another in accordance with the complicated nature of the tidal standing wave and the earth's rotation. In the Poole and Swanage area, where we fish, the range of the tides is very small with an average rise and fall of about three feet. If the sea level

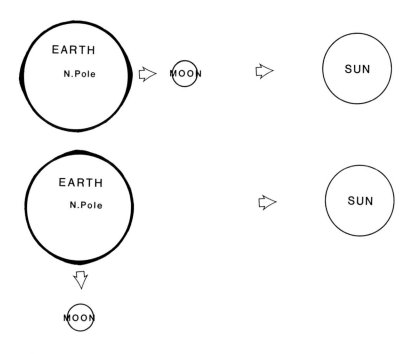

18.   Tides are caused by the rotation of the earth and the attractions of the moon and sun. Spring tides occur when the sun and moon pull in unison or in direct opposition.

was just a little higher and the sea thus extended a little further to
the region of Corfe Castle a few miles inland of Swanage, there
would be virtually no tides at this point.

Because of this small tidal range, bait collecting or digging may
at times be practically impossible. Early in our experience of local
conditions we organised a Boxing Day expedition to fish the
Chesil Beach for cod. The idea was to dig worms on the mudflats
of Poole Harbour just before lunch. The tide tables indicated low
water (neap tides) at about lunch time. We arrived, complete
with digging forks and plastic bait buckets, at about 10 a.m. The
tide was still well in when we arrived but it was a crisp, sunny
morning so we sat down on the turf just above the high water
mark and waited for the ebb to reveal the worm beds, still under

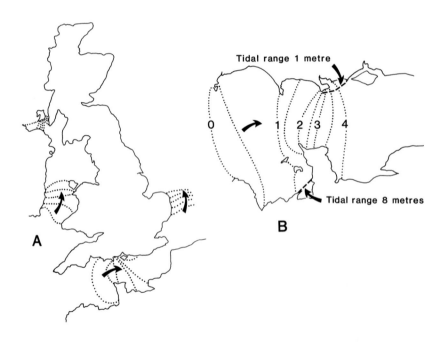

19.   Lines connecting points at which high water occurs at the same times.
A. Note the long delays over short stretches of coast in East Anglia, Dorset,
south-east Eire and the island of Isla (dotted lines show hourly differences).
B. Details of tidal advance up the English Channel (dotted lines show half-hour
differences).

eighteen inches of water. The minutes ticked by with no discernible change in water level. Midday came and went. Perhaps we had misread the tables, surely now the water level would fall, but no - the sea level remained on the upper shore. It was only after four hours of progressively dwindling hope that we got the message and set off for the west, baitless apart from two semi-decomposed squid. We later realised that the strong east wind blowing into Poole Harbour mouth had virtually cancelled out the effects of the weak ebb.

Driving along the promenade at Weymouth it was obvious that not only were there a few acres of (rather sparse) lugworm beds exposed but the recent storms had cast up enormous quantities of weed and rubbish. We parked the car and in twenty minutes were able to dig enough lug and collect enough slipper limpets and spiny cockles to last the entire trip. The subsequent fishing was more or less uneventful, except that as the temperature fell at dusk we had to thaw out the slipper limpets before we could remove them from their shells. Numerous pouting and poor cod plus a single small codling of about 5 pounds were the ultimate results of our ordeal.

Distortion of the advancing tidal bulge by local conditions may have other effects on the pattern of the tides. In our area there is a two-hour delay in the time of high water over just a few miles of coastline. At Poole there is a well-marked double high water. The second high tide is biggest on the neap tides and the first is biggest on spring tides. At Weymouth, along to the west, there is a double low water.

Another very important effect of the rise and fall of water is the creation of strong water currents, almost like rivers flowing within the sea. In coastal regions the main flow will generally be parallel to the trend of the shoreline. The direction of flow will *usually* reverse on the turn of the tide. As in a river, there will be swirls and eddies in bays and around promontories. Since the tide is rising (or falling) most quickly midway between high and low water, it is at these times that the tidal currents will be strongest.

The most obvious difficulty with tidal currents, as far as angling is concerned, is trying to 'hold bottom' with either the tackle or the anchor of the boat. The usual means of combating strong currents are to use wire lines, fancy leads, to fish on the drift, and

so on, and they are dealt with at length in other books on
angling. Our only contribution to this aspect of the tides is in the
use of self-diving spinning lures. It is often more satisfactory to
use a plug which will fish deeper and better in a strong flow than
to add lead to some other form of lure.

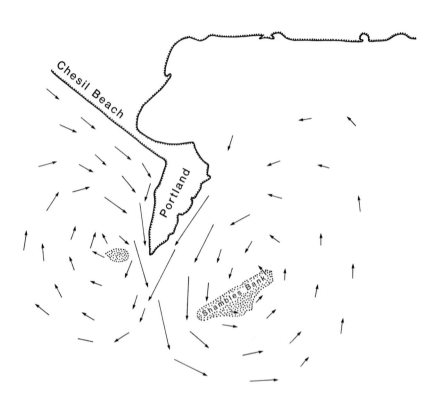

20.   Tidal eddies off Portland create the Shambles turbot bank and its small
counterpart. Similar banks will be found where headlands or islands project
across the tidal flow.

From the boat angler's point of view, one of the most
interesting effects of tidal currents is the creation of banks. These
huge mounds of grit and shell are favoured by some of the more
popular fish species, notably turbot and bass. There are several

well known banks of this type around our coasts and no doubt there are many others still unfished. By chance, the formation of such marks has been studied in detail on the Shambles Bank, a well known turbot ground off Portland on the Dorset coast.

The presence and the position of banks has been shown to be predictable from the directions of the prevailing currents and the geography of the nearby coastline. Headlands, sticking out into the sea, cause different patterns of flow on the flood and the ebb tides. In the huge 'eddies' which result, great masses of coarse sand are dumped on the sea bed. All the finer material is winnowed away by the strong currents and the remaining fragments of shell and gravel are sculptured into giant ripple marks. These are enormous replicas of the ripple marks which we see on the beach and perhaps they can best be visualised as underwater sand dunes. It is in the lee of these dunes that fish like the turbot await their prey.

The largest and best known of such fishing grounds are household names, like the Shambles off Portland and the Skerries off Start Point in Devon. What is less well known is the fact that smaller banks occur more or less as mirror images of the main ones on the opposite sides of the promontories. There must also be many other peninsulas projecting into the tidal flow where similar, if lesser, banks have formed and good fishing potential is untapped. Elongated islands, such as Lundy Island in the Bristol Channel, which lie across the main flow will, of course, create four 'eddies' and banks – two at either end.

The wind blowing over the sea's surface also creates currents of water but these are much less important than the tidal currents. In general, an onshore wind piles up the surface water close to the beach and the result is an undercurrent flowing away from the shore. Offshore winds have the reverse effect and this can be important in pushing surface-drifting food beyond easy casting range.

A much more important effect of the wind from the angler's point of view is the creation of waves. The height of waves is a function of the distance for which a wind has blown over the sea surface (the fetch of the wind). Roughly, a strong wind blowing over four miles of sea surface will build up waves of about three feet high.

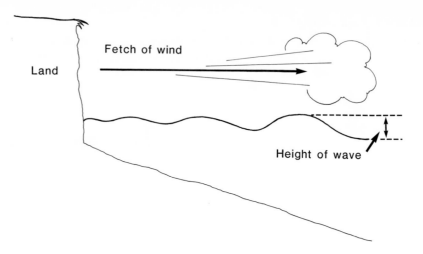

21. Diagram showing how wave height increases with increasing fetch of the wind. Maximum wave height (in feet) = 1.5 times the square root of the fetch in miles.

The active depth of waves (the depth at which they effectively stir up the sea bed) can be estimated as being approximately half the distance between successive waves. Waves breaking along the shoreline are called plunging waves and are caused by the waves feeling the bottom in shallowing water. The other thing that happens to waves as they approach the shoreline is that they tend to slow down and the distances between them become less.

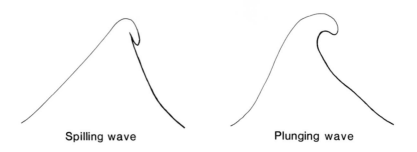

22. Spilling wave caused by shortening wavelength in shallow water and plunging wave (breaker) caused by waves 'feeling the sea-bed'.

However, the height of the waves is not much affected so they become steeper and the tops slide or spill off.

It follows from all this that only along the waterline, or in fairly shallow water, will waves stir up the sea bed to any appreciable extent, even in fierce storms. It is this stirring up which is responsible for uprooting vast amounts of seaweed and for dislodging clinging, hiding or burrowing animals from the sea bed. Under these circumstances fish will often feed avidly on dead or damaged creatures and it is during the period of declining seas after storms that good catches will often be made by bottom fishing with bait in inshore waters.

Since storms are more frequent in late autumn and winter it is essential to take advantage of such events if the best catches are to be made. Cod, conger, bass and large pollack are among the species most susceptible to the beach or dinghy fisherman during these 'falling sea' periods. An oily swell, turbid dirty water and heaps of freshly deposited weed along the tideline are indications of good conditions. Fish normally caught at night may be found feeding actively in the daytime during such periods.

The combined effects of winds, tides and coastal geography are to sort out water-borne materials into masses and to deposit them in characteristic places along the shoreline. Only local scrutiny

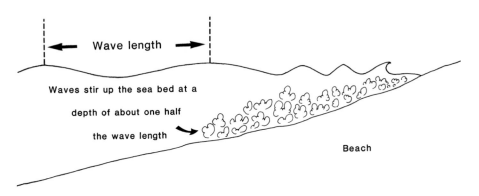

23. Waves normally stir up the sea-bed down to depths of about half-a-wave-length. In water of less than this depth they become steeper and spill or plunge.

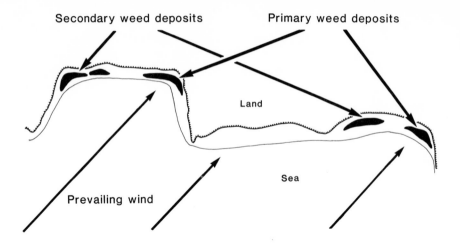

Secondary weed deposits   Primary weed deposits

Land

Sea

Prevailing wind

24. Deposition of weed or flotsam by the prevailing winds blowing onto a rocky shore. Both primary and secondary weed deposits generate maggots and attract fish.

will pinpoint these dumping grounds or dustbins, but generally the greatest quantities of debris will be found in the corners of deep embayments fully exposed to the prevailing winds. Lesser accumulations will be found in lee corners. Surprisingly large amounts of deposited weed can be eroded and removed in a single tide if conditions are suitable, so only by frequent visits to the beach is it possible to keep track of the situation.

5

Life begins at forty

THE GROWTH PATTERNS OF FISH

To many, if not most anglers, the anticipation, though not always the realisation, of catching large numbers of big fish is basic to their enjoyment of the sport. For the sea angler the possibility of catching large fish, perhaps even larger than any previously landed, is ever-present. This element of the unknown is psychologically important to us all.

Just as we live for about seventy years so the maximum age of each fish species is, within fairly wide limits, defined. For example, most pouting have a chance of living for about three or four years (if they are not eaten first) whereas the common skate may survive for up to fifty years. In colder seas a species will tend to grow more slowly, live longer and mature later than in the warmer part of its range. Unlike man, a fish will tend to increase in length and weight more or less throughout its life span. Because of this there is always the chance of catching a fish which, due to its faster growth and/or greater age, is larger than any previously caught.

In this chapter the size, growth and age of a number of fish not considered elsewhere in this book are described as a way of introducing the methods used by scientists for determining these characteristics.

The simplest and most direct method used to assess the growth of fish is to keep them in tanks and to take them out at intervals to be weighed or measured. In his book *The Sea Angler's Fishes*, Kennedy mentions observations of this type on conger eels in large aquaria. These fish grew very quickly and the largest increased from 3-pounds to 90-pounds in only five-and-a-half years. Unfortunately, this sort of growth measurement may give misleading results because of the artificial conditions of such things as temperature, exercise and food supply.

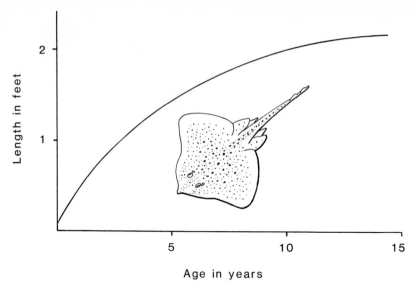

25.   Growth of the spotted ray (aged by tagging).

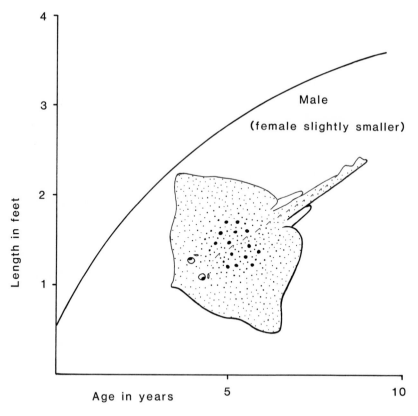

26.   Growth of the blonde ray (aged by tagging).

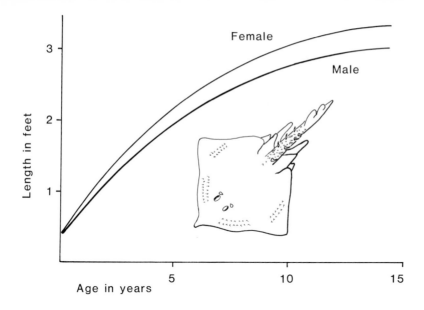

27.   Growth of the thornback ray (aged by tagging).

Similarly direct, and in some ways more satisfactory, is the method in which fish are caught, measured, weighed and tagged before being returned to the sea, the idea being that the fish should be recaptured and remeasured on some future date. Unfortunately, fish may die or be otherwise affected by the tagging procedure, and the chances of catching a given fish for a second time are quite small.

Despite the drawbacks, tagging and recapture methods have been used successfully, particularly in the case of skates and rays. These fish have no bony scales from which the age can be determined. Tagging has shown that males and females of the tiny spotted ray grow at the same rate, both taking fifteen years to attain a length of 2-feet. These rays are often taken in our area when legering with ragworm and small fish-baits. The blonde ray, with which the spotted ray is often confused, is a larger fish altogether and grows much more quickly. The female blonde is slightly smaller than the male but both reach lengths of well over 3-feet in ten years. The well-known thornback grows to roughly the same size as the blonde, but in this species the females are substantially larger than the males. Growth is a little slower than in the blonde and 3-foot long males are about fifteen years old.

A less direct method of ageing has been used on the large common skate, that great 'barn door' of a fish beloved of deep-sea anglers. The vertebral column or back 'bone' of this fish is actually made up of cylinders of cartilage joined end to end. By cutting across one of these cylinders a series of rings is revealed. These rings are similar to those seen on tree trunks and each represents a single year in the fish's life. By counting the rings it

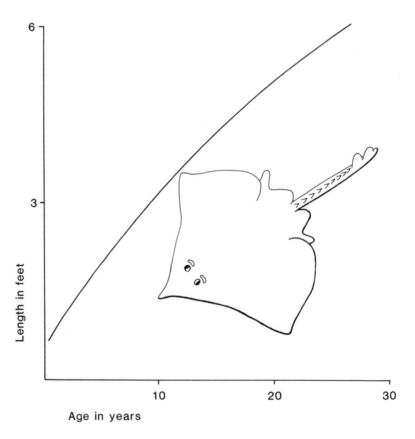

28.   Growth of the common skate (aged by rings on vertebrae). Skate mature at eleven years and live for about fifty.

has been possible to show that the common skate takes about twenty years to reach over six feet in length. These fish do not mature and breed until they are about eleven years of age. As already mentioned, skate of up to fifty years old have been recorded.

The blue shark is an active predatory fish which feeds on herring, mackerel, pilchard, squid, spur-dogfish and even conger. This cartilaginous fish has also been aged by means of the rings in the vertebrae, but to accentuate these annual rings it was necessary to stain them with silver nitrate. Blue sharks grow very quickly so that a ten-year-old fish will be 9- or 10-feet in length. A 12-foot shark may be as much as twenty years old and the diameter of its vertebral column will be about $1\frac{1}{2}$-inches.

A much smaller shark, the spurdog or spiny dogfish, has been aged in a similar manner but in this case it was by counting the growth lines in slices of the second fin spine. Male and female spurdogs grow at about the same rate but the latter lives longer. It

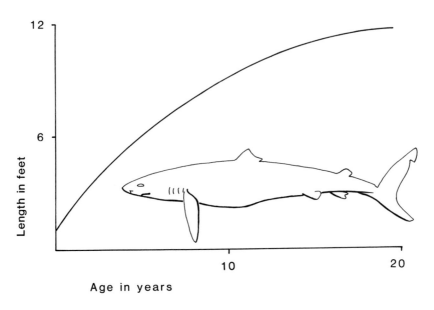

29.   Growth of blue shark (aged by rings on vertebrae). A 12-foot fish may be about twenty years old.

is surprising that a large female spurdog of about 4-feet in length can be almost sixty years old. This great age has also been confirmed by a second, very expensive and extremely laborious method which involves the use of X-rays to detect rings in the vertebrae. The bands thus detected are due to annual deposits of calcium and phosphorus. Using this method it takes about six hours to age a fish of thirty years.

The structures of bony fishes also show annual cycles of deposition, the scaly armour of most being marked with rings

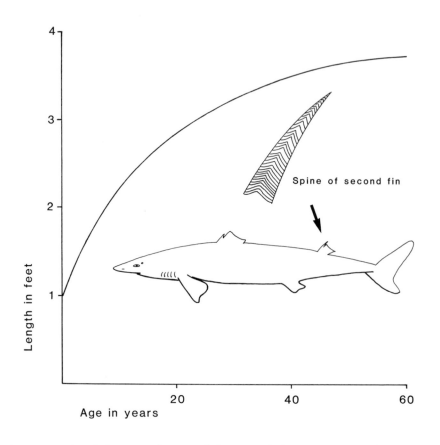

30. Growth of the spur dog (aged by growth lines on second-fin spine). Spurdog live to a great age. They can also be aged by X-ray measurement of vertebrae.

which show a yearly pattern. The pattern on the scale may be due either to alternating periods of fast and slow growth in summer and in winter or to brief checks in growth caused by spawning. In some species the age recorded on the scales is so poor or incomplete that they are of no practical value. In these difficult cases, other structures such as the opercular bone, one of the main bony plates on the gill cover, may provide a superior record of growth and age, also in the form of concentric rings.

Some of the internal structures of bony fish also show an annual cycle of rings or lines. A good example is the otoliths or ear bones, three of which are present within each side of the head. These structures are removed and used for ageing, but the advantage of using scales is, of course, that the fish may be returned alive and the scales will then regenerate. The scales of the thick-lipped grey mullet provide an excellent record of age and growth. Differences in the width of the zones between the scale rings show that these fish grow more slowly in cool summers than in warm ones. Examples of the use of these methods are to be seen in some of the fish dealt with elsewhere in this book.

After being cleaned in boiling water the opercular bones of the bass exhibit a superb set of annual rings. As in the mullet, the width of the rings is greater in warm than in cold years. Being a fish of warmer waters the bass also shows other responses to years when the weather is good. Strong year classes such as those born in 1949 and 1959 originated in years when the sea was warm and there was a preponderance of light southerly winds in the period from May to September. On average, bass which were born in recent years (the 1970s), are smaller *at the same age* than were those born in the 1950s.

The turbot is a flat fish which has no scales and is protected by a tough leathery skin and a few bony lumps on the eyed side. To age turbot the ear bones (otoliths) must be removed and the rings on them counted. In the case of massive, thick ear bones from these or any other fish, it is sometimes useful to grind them down on a slip of carborundum or to snap them across and accentuate the rings by charring them in a flame. The sole and other flatfish are also often aged by this technique.

6

'Who's been swimming on my reef?
PLUGGING FOR BASS

The southern and western coasts of the British Isles are almost at the northern limit of distribution of that superb sporting fish, the bass. As is now well known the bass is a slow-growing fish in this part of its range. Large specimens of 10-pound weight are normally in their late 'teens and twenties. It is an active fast-swimming fish, passing a great deal of time in the shoal water of reefs and estuaries and, at high water, is often found between tide marks within a few feet of the seashore.

There is a great deal of folk lore regarding bass angling, some of which has a foundation of fact based on experience. As will already be apparent, for some years our bass catches consisted primarily of school fish weighing less than a pound. These were, and are, easily taken on legered ragworm from the beaches in and around Poole Harbour, Swanage and Bournemouth. An occasional larger fish of 2 to 4-pounds succumbed to our bait-fishing activities from shingle beaches such as the eastern end of Swanage Bay, Worbarrow and Durdle Door. These fish were pleasing to catch, but because there was no discernible pattern to the catches they gave us little satisfaction in terms of understanding the species.

A little known study by D.B.Carlisle gives a glimmer of insight into the way that bass sometimes behave and, because of this, is of extreme interest to anglers. Carlisle spent many hours observing fish by means of underwater swimming on and around an intertidal reef in South Devon. The reef was inhabited, when the tide was in, by two large bass and seven average-sized thick-lipped grey mullet. The same nine fish came onto the reef each day and were recognisable as individuals by their characteristic scars and damaged fins.

When the tide began to rise, all the fish, bass and mullet,

arrived on the reef *as soon as the water was deep enough for them to swim* (six to nine inches deep). Whether the water was calm or rough the fish came in and they would even travel in with the breaking waves. The two bass came and went individually but the mullet arrived and left as a school. The fish left the reef when the water was still deep, about one hour after high tide *as soon as the ebb current began to run strongly.* Whilst they were on the reef each of the fish kept to its own area. The territories of the mullet overlapped with those of the bass but the two species took no notice of one another. The two bass, however, rarely encroached on each other's area. When undisturbed, the bass lurked in gullies or around the waving fronds of wrack, waiting to pounce out upon passing sand eels or to take shrimps moving on the sandy patches. When a fish was chasing food it kept all its fins folded close to the body until the last instant, when they were spread to act as brakes as the fish turned to seize its prey. In contrast, if a 'strange' bass entered the territory of one of the residents it was driven off by the owner which 'attacked' with fins spread and mouth agape in characteristic threat display.

In this case, at least, the bass were available on intertidal rocks and feeding, even in very shallow water, on most of the flood tide. Since they clocked out an hour after high water, a cessation of bites would be expected then. Also, after catching one or two good bass in the area it would clearly have paid to move on along the beach and fish the next territory, and so on.

Small bass may be found inshore in the south of England throughout most years. The larger fish arrive in spring, essentially for spawning, which takes place in the month of May. Spawning occurs on shallow reefs subject to fast tidal currents, or in shallow estuaries. Bass can adapt without much difficulty to fresh water, but do not usually ascend estuaries beyond the point where crabs and shrimps are abundant. In the autumn and winter large bass tend to leave the vicinity of the shore when the sea temperatures fall from about 13°C to 9°C. On the Irish coast this is in October–November and they return in late April. In Poole Harbour large (double-figure) bass are occasionally taken by netsmen as early as February and March. Sea temperatures are probably the main factor affecting the seasonal migration of bass.

As we have said, our early efforts at bottom fishing with bait produced only school bass and 'accidental' larger fish. The significant events of our first real attempts to catch bass took place in the period 1968-70. Several times Terry and I, both indefatigable spinners, had spent hours spinning from rocks and beaches or trolling artificial baits from hired rowing dinghies. The normal lures used were Toby spoons of various sizes which proved quite effective for mackerel, garfish and small pollack. On two or three occasions, however, much fiercer pulls than those of the usual 'small stuff' had resulted in good fish being hooked and subsequently lost after a couple of seconds contact. These mystery fish were the subject of some speculation but the general view was that they were likely to have been bass. It is possible that the wish was father to the thought.

On one occasion, during a day out at Weymouth with the

Mid-tide level   High water spring tides

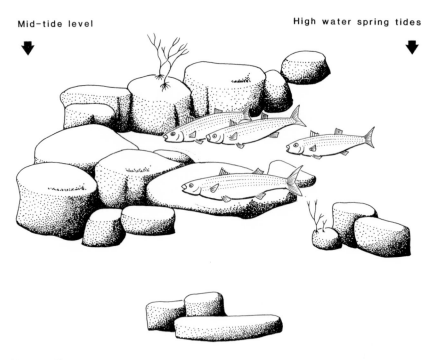

31.   Mullet territories. When disturbed, each mullet leaves its own territory and the fish shoal together.

family, I spent an hour or two on the pleasure pier intent on doing a spot of spinning while the others shopped. The sun was blazing down from a cloudless sky and the pier was crowded with holidaymakers. A big spring tide was ebbing hard and a strong flow of clear, greenish water was leaving the harbour and flowing out between the piers. A few minutes spent peering over the railings, watching other anglers fishing with worm for wrasse and pollack, revealed a steady progression of small shoals of good fish leaving the harbour with the flow. Encouraged, I clipped a small, silver pirk, an ABU Lurette, onto my 10-pound line and cast well out into the fast-flowing water. First cast, as the lure jinked back across the tide, wallop!-a good fish took it and was hooked. After a minute or so of hectic action the fish escaped. Ten minutes later a second fish was hooked and this time was

32. Bass territories. Resident bass chase intruding bass with a characteristic threat display but ignore intruding mullet.

only lost after being played to the base of the pier, where it was clearly seen to be a bass of 5 or 6-pounds. The immediate feeling of disappointment at losing yet another fish on a 'spinner' was slightly tempered by the fact that I knew, this time for sure, that the fish had been a good bass. The bass had been hooked under far from ideal conditions when other anglers using float and bottom tackle were landing only small pollack and wrasse.

The next piece of the jigsaw came from a totally unexpected quarter. Trevor, an angling friend now returned to the north, had been trying, with some success, to catch a 'freezer full' of mackerel for the winter bait supply. He trolled from his small plastic Romany dinghy, powered by a little Seagull outboard. One of the lures which had been used to good effect in these efforts was a small, floating, balsa-wood Rapala plug on leaded trolling tackle. It seemed to some of us that these lures, with their close resemblance to sprats, sand eels and sand smelts, and their tendency to dive and work, even when reeled in slowly against a strong flow, could prove useful when spinning under conditions such as those I had experienced from Weymouth Pier.

On the next trip to Weymouth a brand new medium-sized, green and silver, single-jointed, floating Rapala was in my bag. A visit to a Weymouth tackle shop to buy some new line revealed that the local Ferry Bridge had been reported as fishing well. A quick conference resulted in a change of venue and we asked to be directed to the bridge, anticipating the usual 'you should have been here last week', when we eventually found the place.

We arrived to find that the Ferry Bridge in fact carried the Weymouth-Portland causeway road across the narrow outflow of a huge tidal lagoon, the Fleet, which lies behind the famous Chesil Beach. A hundred yards seaward of the road bridge a rusty and defunct railway bridge, now demolished, also crossed the narrow neck of water. The tide was already beginning to flood and the sea was flowing steadily into the Fleet between the piles of the bridges, gin clear but with the blueness of deep water. Several anglers were already float-fishing or bottom-fishing with ragworm or small prawns from the railway bridge and on enquiry we discovered that they had landed a few small pollack. Shoals of small silvery fish, apparently sand smelts, were clearly to be seen twisting and turning in the shelter of the bridge supports.

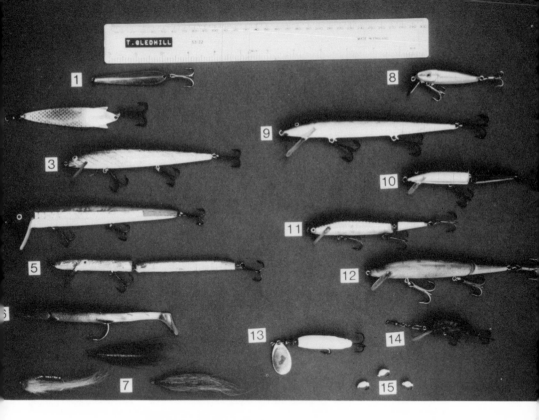

Lures used for bass and mullet fishing

1&2: Pirk and Toby Spoon (used in early days and in deeper water)
3: ABU Killer (one of our first floating plugs. Bass up to $11\frac{1}{4}$-pounds were taken on these lures)
4&5: Home made floaters (Number 4 has taken bass of over 10-pounds and number 5 has proved effective in sizes up to 12" long)
6&13: Redgill and balsa-bodied Mepps (both are useful in dirty conditions amongst bits of floating weed)
8: Small Japanese slow-sinker (used for fry-feeders)
9&10: Rapalas (until recently our most consistent shallow working floaters)
11: The 'Tesco Special' (cheap foreign made floater very effective for bass of all sizes)
12: Rebel J30S, the current favourite. Responsible for many large bass including one of $12\frac{1}{2}$-pounds
14: Rebel crayfish, a recent acquisition useful for bass and with potential as a wrasse lure
7&15: Streamer flies and floating maggot-flies used with a fly rod for bass and mullet

We decided to try spinning from the sandy shore of the boat park which flanked the water between the two bridges. In this way it would be possible to cast our small Toby spoons across the current and fish them round more or less as in a river. Immediately we were into fish, small pollack of $\frac{1}{2}$ to $\frac{3}{4}$-pounds which put up a fair show on our 8-pound lines and light spinning rods. Two hours later our joint catch had topped sixty pollack, all of similar size and all of which were returned to the water.

By now the tide was flowing fiercely through the channel and beginning to flood over the sand on which we stood, making it difficult to control the spinners, or indeed to prevent them skating across the surface. At this stage I remembered my plug—were these not ideal conditions to try it out? I clipped it onto the link swivel and climbed up onto the railway bridge. Most of the other anglers were packing up or had already left because they were

A bass of $8\frac{1}{2}$-pounds with the plug still in its mouth. The free treble hooks are tangled in the net.

unable to keep their tackle down in the fast-flowing water. One chap, on seeing the plug, volunteered the encouraging information that he had never seen anyone catch anything on spinners from the bridge. Never one to be put off easily, I dropped the plug onto the water surface downstream of the bridge and allowed line to peel off the spool as the lure drifted away. After seventy or eighty yards of line had gone, I gave a turn of the handle to bring over the bale-arm and held the rod pointing downwards until the lure had submerged well below the surface. Slowly I began to retrieve, one turn, two turns, wrench! The rod curved sharply over and the check began to give line. The fish boiled on the surface, still seventy yards downstream of the bridge. I played it along towards the point where the rusty ironwork joined the shore and Harry lifted it from the water onto the rocks. A 2½-pound bass! I could not have been more pleased if it had been a record fish. Shortly afterwards the same technique produced a second bass of almost 3-pounds. We talked about them all the way home, our first reasonable bass caught, more or less, by intention.

It was later in the same year that we took the next important step in learning to catch bass consistently. Harry was going with Jim, one or the local postmen, to fish from the boulder-strewn shore of Durlston Bay. Jim, an expert skin-diver and a keen angler, knew a good deal about the local fishing, especially in relation to trolling for bass from his outboard-powered dinghy. The next morning, at work, I could see from Harry's face that their trip had been blessed with success. In fact, the good news was that Jim had caught an 8-pound bass on a small Mepps spoon. The bad news was that he had damaged his ankle in landing it without a net. In trying to kick the fish up the beach he had booted a half-ton cementstone boulder by mistake, effectively putting paid to his shore fishing for the next three months!

Harry, using a No. 2 Mepps Mino, had had four bites and landed one bass of about 3-pounds. It was enough to make the rest of us green with envy.

The following weekend I put my spinning rod into the car after lunch, collected Ian, another member of the group, and drove down to Durlston. It was a superb early summer afternoon and the sun was reflected from the oily surface of a flat calm with only the slightest swell to disturb the wrack cast up along the tideline. Fifty yards from the carpark half-a-dozen anglers were casting a miscellany of floats and tackles at a small shoal of grey mullet which were hanging almost motionless at the surface. Ian succumbed and joined the group, casting his No. 1 silver Mepps repeatedly towards the fish, which appeared totally uninterested in everything.

Never one for crowds, I walked off along the shore 'giant hopping' from one huge grey-yellow boulder to the next. Clearly there was no one else game to walk in the hot sun and the rest of the beach was deserted. I rounded the first prominence of the cliff, every so often making a couple of casts with the floating plug on which I had caught bass at the Ferry Bridge. Every inch of the plug's progress was clearly visible. It wriggled sinuously through the clear water seeming, to me at least, to be irresistible. Although the lure was working well, I had a few qualms about the possibility of deceiving fish, if fish there were, under the bright clear conditions.

Fifty yards further on, the boulders were larger and there was a noticeable change in the sea's edge. The water had taken on the colour of strong tea where the lapping swell was disturbing a huge mass of rotting kelp trapped between the rocks. A swirl in the water two yards out could be just a submerged boulder; there were plenty of them. There was another swirl. I took a few slow steps closer and then I saw them—bass!—and big ones. A dozen or more fish ranging from a couple of pounds up to, perhaps, double figures were grovelling about within a few feet of me. With bated breath I flicked the plug out onto the mirror surface and began to retrieve. One of the smaller fish turned and grabbed it, hooked itself and headed out to sea. I played it along the beach away from its fellows and lifted it carefully from the water. A sharp tap on the head with a handy rock and I was able to unhook it. I returned to the feeding fish and cast again. Three more casts without any sign of interest and I remembered Ian.

I hurried back along the beach and, when I was in view of the aspiring mullet catchers, shouted and waved my arms to attract Ian's attention. Curiously, none of the other anglers took any notice of the excited calls but Ian reeled in and strode along towards me.

A 12½-pound bass taken by spinning from a rocky shore.

We were soon hurrying back to the hotspot. The fish were still there and we exchanged strings of excited superlatives. Ian cast out his small Mepps and it was promptly seized, the little green solid–glass rod bent into a circle and the 6-pound line parted with a sharp crack. The check was set too tightly on the cheap fixed-spool reel. Meanwhile I had hooked another fish, again one of the smaller ones, and was leaping from rock to rock like a kangaroo, with thoughts of Jim's damaged ankle passing through my head as I tried to keep pace with the fish which was running parallel to the beach.

Five minutes later, after I had returned the fish to the water—it was lightly hooked and came off after being beached—I hurried back to find Ian landing a slightly larger fish. 'I've already lost two others,' he called. Having dealt with Ian's bass, a 5-pounder, we turned back to the sea, but the fish were no longer there. Perhaps the ebbing tide had signalled them to leave or perhaps the commotion caused by playing other fish had scared them off. Anyway, we were well satisfied with one fish each to take home and several other bites on Mepps, Tobys and the floating plug.

In the course of that idyllic afternoon, never repeated in exactly the same way since, we had learned quite a bit. We had confirmed the presence of very acceptable bass close in to this rugged, boulder-strewn, wrack-clothed shore. We had shown that sometimes they would take spinners with gusto. The Mepps and Tobys used by Ian seemed to be attractive to the fish, but to prevent them sinking and snagging up on the weed and rocks a foot or two beneath the surface line control had to be perfect. There was no time for overruns or messing about in the very shallow water. The floating plug, in contrast, was attractive to the fish, could be cast quite far enough, and *most important*, could be retrieved as slowly as desired or even left until the occasional 'bum cast' was sorted out.

That trip was the first of many in which we tried to work out the optimum conditions and the best methods for catching bass from the rocky beaches between Swanage and Weymouth. There were obviously two very different alternative approaches. Firstly, bottom, or float fishing, as employed by many other anglers in the area. Secondly, spinning with natural or artificial baits. We already knew from our own observations and the researches of others, that small bass tended to eat shrimps, prawns and ragworm, while larger bass mainly concentrated on crabs and fish.

The stomach contents of the few decent bass we had caught consisted chiefly of shore crabs or, less often, swimming crabs. The latter were not the large, red-eyed, purple-clawed velvet swimmers but the smaller species which live offshore on sandy patches. Anyway, hard crabs of various shapes and sizes were commonly found in the stomachs of bass caught on spinners. The second major item of food was a variety of fish species. Many types of fish were eaten as we later discovered, but strikingly, most were what we subsequently came to think of as 'long thin fish': pipe-fish, fifteen-spined sticklebacks, eels, blennies, rocklings, gobies and dragonets and, occasionally, sand eels. Rarely were sand smelts or young mullet found in the guts, even though the two latter species were conspicuously abundant in and around the areas being fished. One or two other items, more surprising to us at the time, were also noted. The maggots of seaweed flies sometimes filled the stomachs to the exclusion of all else! Large, brown woodlice (*Idothea*) were also present in numbers. In odd instances we found the sort of thing in which angling writers delight but which are of little practical importance: a whole dead mole was in the stomach of a 6½-pound fish, a mass of chicken bones in another good specimen; pebbles, bits of seaweed, a squat lobster and a masked crab were among other items found at various times.

In short, crab was obviously a favourite food but hard-backed crabs have never, to our knowledge, been shown to be useful as bass baits. Soft-backed and peeler-crabs are available locally but, because of the small tidal range, it takes a good deal of time to collect sufficient numbers for a fishing trip. Also, the area in which we were fishing, apart from a few selected spots which were often occupied by other local anglers, was not conducive to bottom fishing without the use of heavy lines and/or the loss of large amounts of tackle.

In view of these difficulties and our recent experiences, we decided that spinning or float-fishing would be our best methods. We tried float-fishing with mackerel strip, squid, and sand eels but under the type of conditions that we were fishing, it never produced as many fish as did spinning. Also, those fish taken on float tackle appeared to be smaller specimens. Because of this we decided to concentrate our efforts on spinning. We make no attempt to comment on the relative merits of crab or other baits and spinners, but the results subsequently obtained by spinning appear to be at least comparable with those of other anglers who bait fish from the same beaches. A brief summarised account of results obtained by ourselves over several years is presented in the final chapter for the reader's own evaluation.

Over a period of months and years following the modest catches already described, a determined effort was made to try out a range of lures for catching bass. The original balsa-wood Rapala was quite good, but, along with the available plastic copies of the time, it had certain disadvantages. All were comparatively expensive, as they still are, and to lose or damage one could be a depressing experience. With practice, losses of lures on snags became minimal, and a lure would often last a season. It was only when fishing over unfamiliar territory that any losses occurred. However, as we soon discovered, most bought lures are easily damaged; the commonest problem being broken diving vanes (lips). These brittle plastic scoops often snapped off, either in playing a fish or in knocking against a rock during casting or retrieving. If the damage was noticed the plug could immediately be replaced by a spare. The most annoying instances of such damage were at dusk, when feeding fish could be splashing and rolling in the shallow water, and it was only after several minutes casting without bites that the damage would be noticed. Plastic lures were also inclined to lose lips, in this case because they were not fixed (glued) into the body adequately. The solution to this problem is simple—a couple of oblique cuts with a saw or hacksaw blade, passing through the base of the lip and into the adjacent body, are filled with a resin glue such as Araldite. The resultant bond is virtually permanent.

A second constructional problem was the loss of hooks, usually because the fixing wire loop (balsa-wood lures) or screw-eye (plastic lures) pulled out in the course of playing or landing a fish or in freeing the lure from a snag. These problems, although uncommon if the hook fixings had been tested by a good pull before use, were unpredictable, annoying and difficult to prevent because they were due to faults in the method of construction or weaknesses of the materials in use.

A third flaw, which was comparatively easy to overcome, was the loss of colour or surface finish. Whether this colour was applied as simple electroplating, paint, enamel or varnished tinfoil, the solution was to give new lures two or three good coats of clear gloss polyurethane varnish. This soon became standard procedure, although there was little evidence that the loss of colour made much difference to the effectiveness of a plug.

Plastic, mass-produced plugs, although generally less well-finished than their balsa counterparts, had certain advantages. Firstly they were harder and thus less likely to be gouged, grooved and damaged, either in the tackle bag or during fishing. Secondly their greater density sometimes helped casting in windy conditions. Only trial and error would reveal whether a particular lure was any good for catching fish, but in general, any long narrow lure of the 'killer' type was worth a try. Plugs of up to ten inches in length were well worth using and there was some evidence that large lures might tend to select for larger fish.

With reference to the last point, on one occasion in the early

1970's I had been using, with some success, a 9-inch, blue-and-silver plastic plug armed with three good-sized treble hooks. The plug was very easy to cast and on a slow, steady retrieve would submerge to a depth of about two feet. Its action was negligible, only the slightest shiver being visible as the lure was retrieved. Harry, finding himself without a plug, came round one evening to borrow my current favourite for an hour or two's spinning from the rocks. The following morning he arrived at my gate before breakfast and beckoned me out into the street. Opening the car boot with a flourish, he revealed a beautiful 11½-pound bass in perfect condition. Then came the bad news—the sea had been rather rough with an onshore wind and the tide was only half-way in. The first cast had produced the large fish which was landed after a five minute struggle. Two casts later my prize lure had snagged on a submerged rock. Despite prolonged efforts to free it, the 10-pound line eventually parted, whereupon Harry had picked up his fish, packed up his gear and returned home.

In view of the various problems encountered in the use of bought plugs an almost inevitable consequence was an attempt to make our own lures. The basic method of construction is shown in Fig. 33. Simple two-jointed models were the standard pattern used, partly because they appeared to behave in a more realistic fashion and partly because one particular joined plastic lure had seemed to be particularly effective, producing thirteen fish for one of our number in his first few weeks of sea fishing

The home-made lures were long, 8 to 10-inches, and rather slimmer in profile than bought versions. The 60-pound breaking strain rustless wire which ran through the centre (glued into a groove sawn along the belly) was bent and twisted from a single piece in each joint, so that there was no possibility of loops pulling out. The hooks were attached by means of split rings so that both hooks and rings could be replaced when rusted or damaged. The lip was of polythene cut from an old bottle, preferably of heavier gauge than the standard detergent container. The rectangle of polythene bottle was glued into a slanting groove sawn in the underside of the balsa-wood of the body. The surface of the lip in contact with the body was roughened up and fixed with Araldite, or similar glue, securing firmly by the method already described. Unfortunately, the flotsam and jetsam on any beach will provide an unlimited range of material for lip construction.

There is considerable scope for deep or shallow diving modifications by varying the angle of the lip and it is also possible to alter the action by altering the width of the lip. A wider lip gives a wilder action. Generally, something like a 45° angle and a width similar to that of the body will be effective. A valuable tip in making *any* plug, gained from the instruction leaflet in Rapala boxes, is that any lure which tends to swim on its side can be corrected by bending the front attachment loop of the plug towards the side which is uppermost in the water. The action of the lure can also be adjusted by bending this loop down (towards the belly) to increase the amount of roll and yaw. In making the lures the wire should protrude far enough from the nose to allow adjustment without being so long as to be easily bent by accident.

A good sand-eel-type finish can be obtained on home-made plugs by glueing a strip of silver paper (aluminium foil) along

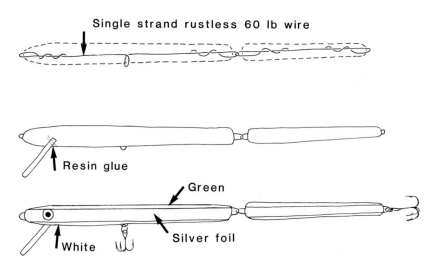

33.   Method of construction for balsa-wood plug.
Stage 1 Loops formed in central wires.
Stage 2 Wire glued into groove along belly and plastic lip fixed with resin glue.
Stage 3 Finished plug.

either side after shaping and smoothing the balsa-wood. The back and belly can then be painted (grey-green and white respectively) and three or four coats of clear gloss varnish added. Models made and coloured in this way have proved to be very effective even when they showed little visible action and retrieved rather like dead sticks. The major drawback with long, jointed, balsa-wood structures is lack of casting weight and high wind resistance. This is less of a handicap than it might appear because, unless they have been disturbed, bass will *frequently* feed within a few feet of the water's edge. These lures have taken fish consistently wherever they have been tried, in Scotland, north-west England, Dorset, Devon and the Channel Islands. A single mid-afternoon's holiday fishing session from the rugged rocks of Corbiére, Jersey, in May produced several 4 to 5-pound bass. Trevor has used home made balsa-wood plugs for catching codling from his small dinghy off the Cumbrian coast. Here is his description of the method just as we received it.

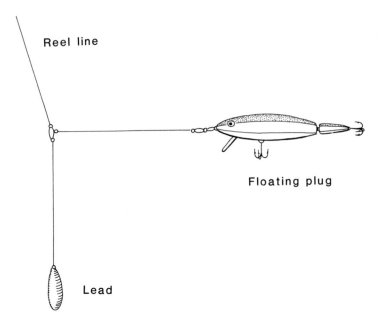

Reel line

Floating plug

Lead

34. Stationary plug rig for cod. In a good flow of tide the fish tend to hook themselves.

(1)   *The plugs*

Home-made imitations after the Rapala pattern. About four to six inches long and just lighter than water. Generally with green backs, silver flanks and white underside. I have used jointed and plain, but the jointed ones seem best. Treble-hooks (not very large) at stern and mid-point.

(2)   *The rig*

As shown in Fig. 34.

(3)   *The gear*

The gear is lowered gently from an anchored boat and set so that the sinker is about one foot above the bottom. Method requires a flow of tide. The plug then 'works' in the current. There is no real need to hold the rod because bites are very positive and I think the fish usually hook themselves.

(4)   *Results*

I have used this method off the Cumbrian coast for codling. Usually the legered plug has been used on a spare rod set up in the stern of the boat whilst my main attention has been given to conventional tackle using bait (lugworm, king rag, mussel, hermit crab).

Bait fishing catches more fish and the fish caught cover a wide range of sizes from around twelve inches long up to about ten pounds, most of them towards the lower end of this range. The 'legered plug' attracts far fewer bites but few bites are 'missed' and the fish caught are almost always of reasonable size (three to ten pounds).

(5)   *Variants*

Codling can also be caught by substituting a small Redgill sand eel for the plug. I have used this set-up off the Galloway coast. 'Sample size' here is smaller, but the general principle that the legered lure attracts less bites than conventionally fished bait but selects for larger fish, appears to hold good.

(6)   *Stomach Contents*

I have cursorily examined stomach contents from Cumbrian codling taken on both bait and lure. The major components of the contents are miscellaneous crustacea (crabs, squat lobsters etc.) with the occasional small fish. The occasional fish turn up more often in stomachs of larger fish than in the stomachs of smaller ones. There is no obvious reason to believe that the codling caught on lures contain more fish than those caught on bait (apart from the size difference already mentioned).

(7)   *General notes*

This method, for obvious reasons, is not very useful unless there is a fair tide running past the anchored boat. However, the same method can also be used for drift fishing or for *very* slow trolling.

Recently, instead of using home made lures we have taken to spinning with American-made 'Rebel' plugs. These come in a great variety of shapes and sizes and have excellent finishes. They are not generally available in this country but may be obtained directly from the manufacturer. The lure which we have used with most success for bass is the J30S. This is a jointed plastic floater $5\frac{1}{2}$-inches long and weighing half an ounce. It casts well even into a strong wind and has a superb action in the water. We have now tested these lures for a full season and taken many good bass including a $12\frac{1}{2}$-pound specimen.

7

Once in a blue moon

BASS FROM THE ROCKS

Shallow, boulder-strewn beaches are liable to produce bass at any time during the period from about late April to mid-November. The time of day and the state of tide seem not to be critical, in the sense that no time is completely hopeless. At first the great majority of our fish were taken within an hour of high water, on the spring tides, when fishing from the open shore. In recent years the actual techniques of fishing have been more or less standard, and most effort has been devoted to extending the periods in which fish could consistently be caught. This was done by experimentally fishing a range of marks under varying tidal and weather conditions. Two examples can be given to illustrate the possibilities.

Freshwater Bay is a broad, gravel beach backed by huge shale cliffs of the type so common in South Dorset. There are submerged rock ledges running out to sea from the beach and much of the bay is extremely shallow with only a foot or two of water a quarter of a mile offshore. This was strikingly brought home to us by Jim, the postman mentioned in the previous chapter. Whilst swimming well offshore he noticed a good sized yacht heading for one of the ledges. It was approaching low water and only eighteen inches of water covered the flat, rock shelf. Unable to make himself heard, he swam as quickly as he could towards the speeding vessel. When he was about fifteen yards away the yacht struck the ledge and immediately there was panic. People appeared from below decks shouting and donning life jackets. Jim swam slowly alongside and, in his rich Dorset voice said 'Afternoon' and then stood up. The water scarcely covered his knees.

Significantly, only a short distance east of the bay lies St Aldhelm's Head, a massive, limestone headland with an associated tide race of the type in which bass are known to spawn. In May and June, during and after spawning, large bass are apt to spend a great deal of time in and around the shallow bays adjacent to the race; bays which in calm, sheltered conditions provide a haven for countless young fish.

Our first indication that good bass were to be taken from such situations came from a lone foray by Jon Bass (truly, that is his name), one of our group who is, by inclination, a fanatical freshwater match fisherman and, by nature, a first-rate observer of fish behaviour. Jon, on an exploratory walk with rod and balsa plug, ventured along the shores of Freshwater Bay. He was looking more than fishing, casting and retrieving occasionally as he went. To cut a long story short, Jon had a bite and hooked a good 8-pound bass. As he played the fish in the calm clear water he could see two other fish, of similar size, swimming alongside, probably still with spawning in mind. Having beached the fish Jon quickly unhooked it, cast again and promptly hooked and eventually lost one of its partners.

A couple of days later saw Harry and I parking the car in the cliff top carpark at Chapman's Pool. The usual 10-foot spinning rods, Cardinal reels and 8-pound lines were put together. Floating plugs were tied on and hooked onto the butt rings in preparation for the forthcoming walk. Down the winding track alongside the small stream we went, brushing through the overhanging thickets of blackthorn, still with the odd white flower, over the cracked earth of the landslips which scar the coombe leading down to the sheltered waters of Chapman's Pool.

The 'Pool' itself is a good spot for mackerel in late summer and for conger when the sea is rough and coloured. Crossing the slippery grey mud, where the little stream disgorges its water onto the beach, we rounded the curve of the shingle beach under the shadow of the tall crumbling cliffs. The tide was out and still falling slowly towards low water. The sun blazed down onto a clear sea which sparkled brilliantly as the faintest of breezes ruffled the surface. Through a series of little gravelly bays we trudged and over the rough-surfaced limestone blocks which litter the points between. Off came the Barbour jackets as the sweat ran down our faces and we plodded on. The first view of Freshwater Bay itself was a revelation. The wide sweep of the bay was backed by massive dark grey cliffs, fronted by a steep pebble beach. At the near end of the beach was a large wooden pontoon, torn loose from a nearby cove where it had formerly been used as a diving platform. It lay half in the water amidst a mass of loose weed. The broad beach was scalloped into a series of little shingle bays and points. A tiny stream trickled down the face of the cliff at the back of the beach and disappeared amongst the stones. At the far end of the bay, a plume of spray marked the descent of another stream over the cliff edge.

We stopped walking to have a breather and to survey the scene. Patches of tiny ripples dappled the smooth blue-grey surface of the bay. Opposite the point where we had stopped, and about two hundred yards out in the centre of the bay, one patch of ripples seemed more persistent than the others. Our attention became focused on the patch and together we exclaimed, 'That was a fish!' A rounded grey back broke the surface of the water, and another. 'At this range they must be good-sized fish or we would never see them; what do you reckon, Harry? I suppose they must be bass,' I said. 'They couldn't be anything else,' replied Harry. 'Pity they're so far out, perhaps they'll come in later.'

We walked on towards the beach and Harry continued the conversation. 'They must be damned great fish to be visible at that distance.' 'What's the best plan of action, do you think?' I asked. 'We can split up and work along the beach from either end. Give me a shout if you get one,' said Harry, and he set off along towards the waterfall, taking care to keep well back from the water's edge. Half-an-hour passed as, casting and retrieving the plugs, we worked our way along the four hundred yards of beach. Like a double-sized mirror image, Harry approached me from the far end of the shingle and we were within a rod's length of one another when he hooked a bass of about 2½-pounds. I stood behind him as he beached it, unhooked it and returned it to the sea. 'Have you noticed that shoal of fish? I reckon they're coming closer; they seem to be heading for the corner where that old pontoon is,' said Harry. 'O.K. Let's work our way back there, it must be just about low tide.' As we approached the corner of the bay an incredible sight met our eyes. The clear water was alive with brit of about an inch or two in length and now, about

The large mouth of a 7-pound bass. Typically, the fish is hooked in the corner of the mouth on the middle treble.

fifty yards out, the swirls and boils of feeding bass were very obvious and rapidly coming closer. Soon we could see fish of up to 10 to 12-pounds careering about, only a yard or two from the margin of the sea and gulping in the little fish as though every bite was their last. We cast and cast again, but apart from a 3-pounder on Harry's plug we had no other bites. We were becoming frustrated; clearly the bass were preoccupied with the brit. We rummaged through the tackle bags. There were plenty of big plugs but, of course, nothing small enough with the possible exception of a 3-inch, blue and silver plastic wiggler, which I had bought to use for salmon. The plug was a very slow sinker with a metal lip and two very sharp, nickel-plated, trebles—excellent considering that it was such a cheap lure. First cast with the little plug and I was into a good fish which tore out to sea and away along the beach. The bass was clearly visible in the clear water and took about five minutes before it could be slid onto the beach and lifted, fingers in gills, taking care to avoid the trebles in its mouth. Back in the corner Harry, one of the world's most persistent anglers, was still casting and retrieving without success. I returned, cast again and immediately was into another good fish. The procedure was repeated as before and it soon became clear that, apart from the brit, the little plug was the only thing the bass would take.

As dusk fell and the tide began to flood the bass again moved out and by mutual agreement we 'gave it best' and turned to look at our catch. With slight feelings of guilt we realised that there were twelve fish lying on the beach, apart from the other ten or twelve smaller bass which we had returned to the sea. The catch ranged from 4 to 10-pounds with a total weight of well over seventy pounds.

'How the hell are we going to get these back?' said Harry. 'With difficulty, I should think. There's an old pole back there, let's sling them on that.'

We collected the pole which was about six feet long, streaked with oil and at one end decorated with a bunch of stalked goose barnacles picked up as it drifted in the Atlantic. We threaded the fish via their gills and mouths along the pole and then sat down for a five-minute breather before the long trek back.

Now that we had time to take stock we noticed that out hands were trembling like leaves. We stared at the fish and turned our heads slowly until we were looking one another in the eye. 'Once in a blue moon!' I muttered and Harry, probably for the only time in his life lost for words, simply nodded his head. It was dark as we trudged and stumbled the two miles back to the carpark in almost total silence, both feeling the satisfaction which comes after a good fishing trip.

At the obligatory 'inquest' the following morning we considered what had been learned from this success. Low water neaps and calm, clear conditions in late spring and summer cause brit to shoal up in very shallow water close to the shore. The bass, when they are preoccupied with small fish, are difficult to catch except on a 'small fish' imitation. We had no doubt that a tube or streamer fly would have been at least as effective as a small plug, but it was not until later years that fly fishing became one of our regular methods for catching both bass and mullet.

Subsequently, we took many good bass from 'Pontoon corner'

Four bass caught by spinning with Rebel plugs. Note the fly rods, always carried in case fish are feeding on seaweed fly maggots or fish fry.

as we came to know it, even though two years later the pontoon disappeared, as no doubt it had arrived, in a winter storm. Often, at low water of both neap and spring tides, good bass can be seen foraging along such shingle beaches in the waves which are breaking on the shore. These fish are usually in ones and twos and great care must be taken so as not to scare them, particularly in calm, clear conditions. Usually the first sign of a fish will be the swirl in the water's edge as it sees the angler and swims away. The best tactics to adopt in these conditions, require a very quiet approach along the beach moving in the same direction as the tidal current. The fish will then be approaching the angler, face to face, as they swim uptide against the flow. Every few yards a series of casts should be made starting with the first parallel to, and only a couple of feet from, the water's edge and then covering the water in a fan-like manner. If, as is often the case, there has been wind or rain and the sea is coloured with stirred up sediment or mud washed in from the land, it probably pays to cast more or less directly out to sea, moving a few yards along the beach after every half-a-dozen casts. In the course of an hour or two, quite long stretches of the shoreline can be covered, particularly by two or three anglers working to a system. Usually a tide will only produce one or two bass in these conditions but they will often be good fish of over 5-pounds weight.

Apart from the basic spinning technique, using the floating plug, we have tried a variety of other methods. Many of these approaches have produced fish, but none with the consistency of plug fishing. Peeler crab used in coloured water has, on several occasions, resulted in reasonable catches of smaller bass but, according to the published accounts of other anglers, it is clearly capable of better results. Similarly, using squid, both legered and float fished, we have had the odd bass, some of good size. Frozen sand eel, the only form in which this bait is readily available to us, is productive in both clear and coloured water, and in fact one of the best bass which we have so far taken, a fish of $12\frac{1}{4}$-pounds, was caught on a legered 'eel' as the sea settled on the day following a violent August storm.

On the principle that natural baits should be more attractive to large fish than are artificials (certainly true with the pike that we fish for) we have spun with dead dace, our most easily obtained

Spinning from a rocky ledge in a south-westerly gale in November. Shortly before the picture was taken seven good bass were caught in three-quarters-of-an-hour.

little silver fish. This method resulted in a number of 'takes' but, for some reason, the bass tended to drop them rather quickly.

Mackerel strip is a bait widely used by local anglers legering for bass, and decent specimens are at times taken by those 'in the know', usually at the cost of a certain amount of bottom tackle. Of necessity, bottom fishing on the snaggy terrain which is often associated with good bass catches is a rather static business. Because of this static element it is not compatible with the searching approach, which enables the angler to locate small, scattered concentrations of feeding fish. This is particularly important when fishing time is limited.

On the rather few trips when fishing a floating plug fails to produce bass, other species will often fill the breach. Pollack, sometimes good fish of 4 to 6-pounds weight, will be found feeding in (to us) surprisingly shallow water. This is particularly true at dusk, when the anticipated fierce initial pull of a bass sometimes turns into the tearing bite, powerful dive and subsequent rather disappointing fight of the pollack. If pollack are the fish in mind, it is usually most productive to fish from rocky ledges into rather deeper water over thick beds of kelp or wrack. Good bags of pollack were often the result of trips to such venues as Winspit, Tilly Whim and Worbarrow Tout, but we have not done enough of this fishing to have observed any consistent pattern in the catches made. On one day the fish caught will be so small that the plug which takes them is longer than they are. Other trips may be blessed with two-year-old $\frac{3}{4}$-pounders and these may suddenly be replaced by larger fish of 2 or 3-pounds in weight. The deeper water usually necessitates the use of a weight up trace of the plug. The exception is the dusk period when even large fish will take at the surface, swimming smartly up from the weeds to take the plug and crash diving back to their retreat. Rather than resort to the use of lead it is sometimes better to fish with a Redgill eel, Eddystone eel or even a Toby spoon or pirk if the water is very deep.

Over deep water, particularly during prolonged spells of hot, calm, summer weather, mackerel will also take the plug well although if these fish are present it is usually time for a change to a Mepps or a small silver spoon, the weight of lure being adjusted in accordance with the distance which it is necessary to cast.

Wrasse of all sizes are liable to take plugs used for bass. Immediately following the wholesale wrasse deaths which took place in the hard winter of 1962-3 the larger ballan wrasse which we caught were all taken while spinning for bass. This was despite many hours spent fishing with worm or hard crabs at the same venues and the fact that numerous smaller wrasse were caught by these methods. Wrasse of all sizes generally seem to lunge out from the cover of wrack or kelp and nip at the tail of the passing plug. In this way they are normally hooked in the lips by the rear treble of the lure. A wrasse of 3 or 4-pounds can give a creditable imitation of a bass until the handsome, mahogany-coloured flank comes into view.

Grey mullet, both large and small, will take plugs, particularly under late autumn conditions of rough and coloured water. The bass and mullet are often found in association on the same shore marks but their approach to moving lures is quite different. The bass normally turns and slams into the lure from the side or totally engulfs it from behind, but the mullet, *if and when it shows any interest at all*, follows cautiously behind and merely plucks at the tail end. As a result of this behaviour the mullet, like the wrasse, is invariably hooked in the lips by the tail treble.

In conclusion, it is perhaps worth recounting a more recent bass fishing experience which illustrates that there is still room for a considerable improvement of catches based on the spinning tactics described. Usually, in the presence of large amounts of loose, drifting seaweed, plugs with their treble hooks are virtually impossible to fish. In these circumstances we would normally resort to a Redgill preceded by a yard trace tied to a swivel. The Redgill's single hook is less likely to fall foul of weed and the uptrace swivel sweeps up the odd bits before they reach the lure. The tail of these lures continues to wag even when the hook is fouled. However, this is not always the answer as we have now discovered.

It was in the middle of November; Jon Bass and I had been running a series of evening classes on sea angling in Weymouth and intended to conclude the course with a practical fishing trip to Pinder's Corner. Subsequently the class gathered in the carpark, having brought along a variety of rods, reels, tackles and baits and were well prepared for the weather. They needed to be. On arrival the wind was howling in, at a good force eight, from the south-west. On the beach, fully exposed to the weather, the surf was roaring in from three or four hundred yards out. The water was filthy and full of drifting weed, virtually unfishable. To salvage something from the day we decided to try to find a sheltered spot. After a little discussion and a long walk we arrived to find the sea reasonably calm in the lee of a jutting angle of cliff, but mountains of 'uprooted' kelp lay in the sea's edge. Everyone set about their respective method of fishing in the opaque water. The results surprised even the class tutors. Two small bass taken on legered lugworm and squid were not too much of a shock, but a $7\frac{1}{2}$-pounder on a ragworm float fished by a young woman pupil made the day. In addition to the fish caught, two or three good-sized bass were seen swimming in and around the outer fringes of the drifting kelp. A series of trips to the same spot later that year produced no more fish and the event was mentally filed and put down as a fluke organised by some angling deity overlooking the affairs of evening classes.

It was in fact some years later that the significance of the event was revealed when I made another November excursion, on my own this time, to the same area. As I drove across the grass of the cliff-top carpark, the first smell of well-rotted wrack drifted in through the open car window. Outside the car a stiff onshore breeze was blowing from the south-west and a typically grey November sky was reflected in a leaden sea. I put on the old Barbour jacket, no longer waterproof, tucked my trouser bottoms in my socks and pulled on the old waders, still damp inside from the previous day's rainy pike fishing trip.

I put up my 10-foot Legerlite spinning rod, attached the Cardinal 77 reel with a spool of new 9-pound B.S. Kroic nylon and tied on a small link swivel to which I clipped a 6-inch, jointed floating plug. A couple of spare plugs were slipped into my pocket. Then there was only the old gaff to sling on my back and the door locks of the car to check before I set off down to the shore.

I slipped and slithered down the muddy steps to the beach, a strip of cobble-strewn grey shale at the base of crumbling cliffs. The neap tide was well out and little waves of shallow turbid water were racing onto the shore driven by the strong wind. Recalling the evening class trip made under not dissimilar conditions, I set off on the mile walk over shifting cobbles. The smooth rocky tables were treacherous with an invisible film of microscopic plant cells and there were huge slabs of cementstone fallen fifty feet from the cliff face. I was heading for that tiny sandy corner which I hoped would again be reasonably sheltered.

Approaching the twenty yard strip of gritty sand, I saw that the water's edge was choked with a mass of kelp torn free by the previous month's storms. The band of kelp bits was five or six yards wide and surged gently to and fro on the incoming swell. A swirl at the edge of the surging brown weed showed that there were bass in the sandy water just beyond. Wading knee deep in the weedy margin it was soon obvious that there were many fish hidden by the two feet of dirty water. Here and there a humped grey back was breaking the water, both dorsal fins depressed. Two yards to my left a large pale-grey tail with the rounded lobes characteristic of a bass, waved slowly above the surface as its owner grubbed on the bottom.

The plug was cast five or six yards beyond the feeding fish, a couple of quick turns of the reel took it below the surface and then it wriggled its way back to the rod. For an hour or more I cast and retrieved; many times the lure 'swam' within inches of a fish's snout and every time it was ignored. Even more often the treble hooks dredged up a piece of drifting weed and the light plug came in stone dead. Just as my attention began to wander a sharp tug on the rod top was followed by a screech from the reel and a fish plunged away before shearing round towards the rocks on the left. Within seconds it was obvious that the fish was not very large, a few seconds more and a lift of the rod slid it over the loose weed, a flapping, kicking bar of silver. A 2-pound bass is scarcely big enough to keep but this one was too well hooked and the combination of leathery mouth, treble hooks, spiny fins and gill covers and lively fish, was too dangerous to handle. Even after the fish had been despatched, strong pliers were needed to remove the trebles, the front one from the scissors and the tail one from the base of the pelvic fin. The fish was carried up the beach, well out of reach of the waves and laid close to a conspicuous boulder so that it would be easier to find.

Back at the water's edge I began to cast again. On the third cast a gentle pull was followed by a sharp strike which resulted in another hooked fish. This time the struggle was more prolonged but the fish adopted the same tactics as its predecessor, kiting round to the left and in towards the beach. As it lay on its side held on a short line in the outer edges of the kelp litter, to my horror the hook popped out of its mouth. Dropping rod and reel on top of the weed I stooped and, using both hands, flung the unfortunate bass up the beach. A fine satisfying fish of $4\frac{1}{2}$-pounds.

A further hour-and-a-half of fishing produced no further bites and the autumn dusk was beginning to fall. 'Ah well,' I muttered. 'Just a couple more casts.' On the next cast a dragging pull on the rod top was answered by a tentative strike and the water boiled two yards out as a good fish felt the hook. This time I was prepared for the rush to the left and in towards the floating weed for shelter. Already with the rod held high I stumbled through the shallow water and clinging leathery straps, tripping and slipping as I went, but the fish was too powerful. By the time I had come abreast of it, the bass was already nosing under the weed and boring further and further from the open water. The line juddered round the floating fronds and at any instant I expected the hook to give way. Now the fish was almost at my feet. Slipping the gaff off my back I pulled the piece of rubber tubing from its point with my teeth, and quickly gaffing the fish and flicking open the bale arm of the reel, I carried it up the beach to safety. An 8-pound fish, hooked neatly in the corner of the mouth. It was a perfect end to a fine afternoon.

The stomachs of the three fish caught under these conditions proved to be stuffed with large, red-brown, marine woodlice (*Idothea*). In view of this preoccupation it was hardly surprising that so few bites were forthcoming. In fact on two similar trips in the same month, despite the presence of numerous feeding bass, we obtained not a single bite on worm, peeler crab, squid, plug or Redgill. On any recurrence of similar conditions, float-fished 'lice' or possibly a large wetfly will be our next approach. Already many bass have taken flies in the course of our combined bass/mullet trips and some details of these methods will be given in the chapter on grey mullet.

8

The 'gay' cleaners

FISHING FOR WRASSE

In the way that many freshwater anglers 'cut their teeth' on the humble perch, a free biting and attractive fish, sea anglers, certainly in the south and west of the country, are often initiated into the sport by catching wrasse.

Since we began fishing in Dorset we have caught considerable numbers of wrasse from rocky places between Swanage and Portland. Good fish have been taken on a wide variety of baits, with hard crab being the favourite. Our two largest wrasse (about 6-pounds each) were caught on legered lugworm fished close to the rocks over a bottom of sand and stones. Significantly, this particular catch was made in a turbid sandy sea following a violent storm.

We have never specialised in wrasse fishing and it would be pointless to go on at great length about a subject that other anglers can write upon with more authority. However, we feel that the following information could be of interest to all wrasse anglers.

The common species of wrasse, the corkwing and the larger and more desirable ballan, are rarely to be found very far from rocks and weed. The ballan wrasse, although it is such a common fish, has many interesting features related to its life and habits. When these wrasse mature at an age of about six years, they are females. Subsequently, somewhere between the ages of seven and fourteen years they change sex so that all large ballan wrasse are males.

In the waters off the Isle of Man ballan wrasse grow very slowly and live for up to about thirty years. A twenty-nine-year-old fish is about twenty inches in length, whilst one of $3\frac{1}{2}$-pounds in weight could be as much as twenty-five years old. They can be aged by means of the annual rings on their opercular bones. The growth pattern is very unusual as there is no apparent decrease in the rate with age. A 5-pound fish from the Dorset coast appeared to have grown much more quickly than those from the Isle of Man.

The tough rubbery lips with their many grooves and folds, the strong flattened teeth and the powerful grinding throat teeth are all indications that these fish favour a rather crusty diet. The wrasse has no stomach and the length of its gut suggests that it is an omnivore with catholic tastes. However, ballan wrasse tend to be carnivorous with shore crabs, edible crabs and squat lobsters the main items of food, particularly in the larger fish. Marine 'woodlice' are of secondary importance and the superbly coloured

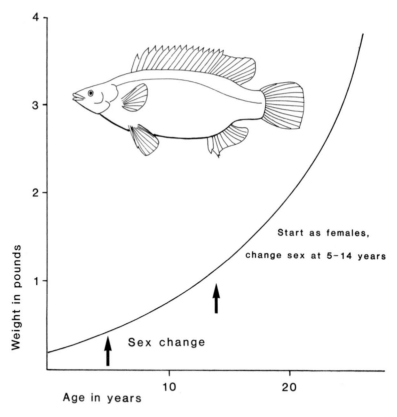

35.   Growth of the ballan wrasse off the Isle of Man (aged by opercular bones). Fish grow slowly and live for up to 29 years.

The mouth of a 5½-pound ballan wrasse caught on a Rebel crayfish plug.

little blue-rayed-limpets and various winkles third. Lesser quantities of brittle-stars and barnacles are also eaten. Very few fish or algae are taken. The ballan wrasse feeds offshore from about March to June but is inshore for the rest of the year. Feeding activity is much less in winter than in summer when after spawning in June the intensity of feeding increases sharply to reach a peak in August.

In fishing for wrasse it is well known that fish baits are generally ineffective. Worms will attract fish of all sizes but tend to select for the smaller specimens. On the other hand, in line with the natural diet of the fish, hard crabs, whole or in pieces are superb baits for larger wrasse. All wrasse are essentially daytime feeders and the onset of dusk usually heralds the cessation of bites from these fish.

The usual problem encountered in fishing for wrasse is that of snagged and broken tackle. Not only does their rocky habitat

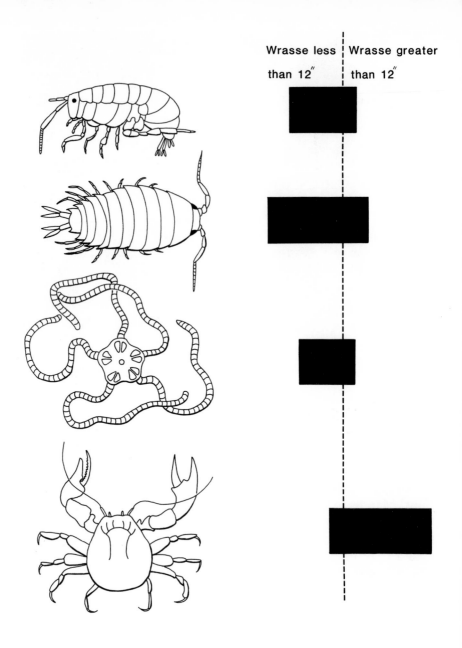

36. Food of the ballan wrasse. Larger wrasse tend to feed on crabs and squat lobsters.

1. Edible crab
2. Shore crab
3. Squat lobster (blue and orange species)
4. Slaters
5. Blue-rayed limpet
6. Brittle star
7. Long-spined sea scorpion (Bullhead fish)

TABLE 5   Foods of ballan wrasse roughly in order of importance.

entail fishing in heavily weeded conditions but the wrasse themselves react in a characteristic and annoying fashion when they are hooked, by taking refuge in the nearest crevice. The outcome of this behaviour is that a successful strike, following a good bite, is often greeted by total immobility, followed by loss of end tackle. Sometimes, though not as often as one might hope, heavy tackle will enable a fish to be hauled from its hiding place. In general the strength of the line is not too important, provided that it will withstand a certain amount of abrasion from rocks, barnacles and the teeth of the fish. Usually it is necessary to adapt tackle and line-strength to the venue. Over rough rocks with innumerable holes and cracks, even small fish will frequently make good their escape. If, by contrast, the rock surfaces are comparatively smooth and the weed is not too dense, even large wrasse, which are not dogged fighters despite their chunky build,

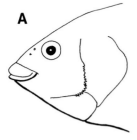 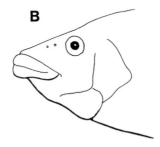

37.   Comparison of the heads of (A) corkwing and (B) ballan wrasse. The former has a saw-edged pre-opercular bone.

Corkwing (lower) and ballan wrasse. Fish lice are visible on the skin of the larger fish.

can be landed on 10- or 12-pound B.S. lines.

Corkwing wrasse will frequently be caught when fishing with worm for ballans. They are rather more colourful than the ballan wrasse which they otherwise resemble quite closely, but they are easily distinguished by the saw-edged pre-opercular bone, on the gill-cover. A large proportion of the corkwings which we catch have, on the shoulder, a characteristic lump, rather like a boil, caused by the presence of a parasite under the skin.

Another interesting aspect of wrasse behaviour is that of cleaning other fish. In much the same way that birds pick leeches from the mouths of crocodiles and ticks from the backs of antelopes, the corkwing wrasse has been observed to clean parasites from the skin of the red bream. The tiny goldsinny and rockcook wrasses also behave as cleaners for larger fishes, as do certain pipe fishes.

Ballan and corkwing wrasse are also unusual in their breeding habits. In the period from June to July they construct nests of algae which they wedge into rock crevices.

9

'You gaff it!'

CONGER FROM THE BEACH

I rang Harry's door bell and found him ready to go. A flask was filled with his characteristic and peculiar brew of coffee—hot, wet and undrinkable (according to his fishing partners). He had on his standard winter gear—two pairs of trousers which obviously doubled for painting apparel, two pullovers, tatty Barbour coat and well-worn waders. His two rods were carefully propped up against the wall of the garage alongside his trusty angle-iron rod rest, his gaff and the tackle bag, an army relic. We were off for an evening's conger fishing from the beach at Durdle Door.

By the time the tackle was packed into my small blue Viva there was hardly room enough for us, but we squeezed in and set off on the twenty-minute drive through the Purbeck hills. Arriving at the carpark we flashed our parking ticket at the man on the gate and drove on over the 'sleeping policemen', through the caravan site and into the field which serves as a parking place. No other cars were in the field so it seemed likely that we would have the beach to ourselves apart from the odd (sometimes *very* odd) holidaymaker. We unloaded all the gear, put the rods together and began the long descent to the sea.

The stiff wind was wailing through the tall dark pine trees on the camp site but it was not strong enough to make fishing difficult. At the edge of the enormous ridge which separates Durdle Door from Man o' War Bay, we paused, looking down at the sea. A heavy swell was welling through the rocky archway and swinging onto the beach where it broke in a short, steep surf. 'Looks good,' muttered Harry and then we started to descend the steps cut into the cliff and clearly designed for giants of years past. After the recent rains the steps were slippery with sticky brown clay. It was now quickly approaching dusk and there were still about three hours before high water. In the dim light we each set up one rod armed with 10-pound line, 1-ounce of lead and a small hook baited with ragworm, in an attempt to catch some pouting for bait. The other rods were also assembled with 18 to 20-pound lines, running legers and 2-ounce pyramid leads. The traces were 15 inches of 30-pound B.S. nylon-covered wire armed with 4/0 bronzed, eyed hooks, well sharpened and baited with frozen squid. I was using fixed spool reels, two ABU Cardinal 77's while Harry had multipliers, an Ambassadeur 5000 and a 7000.

As we waited for darkness to fall we laughed about our previous trip which had resulted in an amusing encounter with a holidaymaker. It had been a warm still night and we were sitting, rods rested, awaiting a run from a conger, much as we might have done when after carp at one of the local clay pits. The parallel between carp and conger fishing had often struck us. As we sat, a middle-aged gentleman wandered along the beach with an extremely small dog running to and fro and sniffing around at his heels. The dog, being of an inquisitive nature, noticed us and ran on ahead to inspect. After examining my bait-stained haversack the dog cocked his leg and proceeded to make his mark on both bag and contents. 'That's lucky,' said Harry. 'What the . . . . . do you mean, lucky!' I responded. 'It could have been my bag,' said Harry. With that I turned to the owner of the dog who had now approached. 'Your dog has just . . . . . . all over my fishing bag,' I said. 'If he is still here in one minute's time I shall put him on this . . . . . . hook for bait!' The dog-owner took one look at my unshaven countenance illuminated by the last rays of the setting sun, picked up the dog, tucked it under his arm and ran like a gazelle up the cliff steps.

An hour had now passed since our arrival; Harry had a bite on the worm and reeled in a small pouting. A head and two fillets of pouting make three good baits. We fished on and quickly caught a couple more pouting before changing over the two 'bait rods' to conger tackle. All four rods were then baited with freshly caught pouting and recast. Two were rested with the reels on a light check and the other two hand held. By this time it was pitch dark with a dense cloud cover hiding the rising full moon. All was quiet so we each poured a cup of coffee and continued our discussion of previous trips.

Night-time conger fishing from a shingle beach.

We recalled the night when the sea had been exceptionally rough; even Harry's 4-ounce lead was rolling around and yet I seemed to be having no trouble holding bottom with my 2-ounce. I smiled and chaffed my partner every time Harry wound in and cast again. Finally Harry said, 'Where's your line and lead? I'll try to cast somewhere near it.' He switched on the torch and followed the angle of my line—only to find that I had cast further than I thought and that my lead was wedged part way up the cliff on the far side of the little bay.

It was on a similar rough night that we had had one of our most spectacular catches. Trevor had a 'conger' run and struck into a powerful 'fish'. He played it carefully in the heavy surf and strong undertow. Back and forth we went along the beach for about fifteen minutes. At last, with Trevor having regained most of the line, Harry had advanced cautiously towards the pounding surf, gaff at the ready and torch in the other hand, only to collapse with laughter. 'Don't laugh—gaff it!' shouted Trevor. 'You gaff it!' said Harry, and Trevor approached to discover that the monster was a British Rail reject sleeper, giving a good simulation of a conger in the drag of the undertow.

Back on the beach things were still quiet. Now it was only about an hour before high water and we were imbibing more horrible coffee. Suddenly there were a couple of clicks from the reel on one of the rested rods. Signs of action at last! A few more clicks and then there was a steady pull of about a foot of line from the reel. As quickly as he could Harry reeled in the other three sets of gear; there was no point in risking any crossed lines. I was holding my rod now and the fish was moving off again. I carefully set the slipping clutch on the reel and struck hard, taking three steps back as I did so. The rod bent over and a fish was on. The line was dragged off against the resistance of the clutch as the fish swam away parallel to the steep gravel beach. I followed, struggling along over the loose, rounded stones, but the fish turned and swam back to where it was hooked. 'It's a good fish,' I shouted over the noise of the breaking waves. More line was torn from the reel. At last the conger was tiring and I pumped it in, yard by yard, towards the beach. 'I'll bring it in on the next decent wave,' I said. Harry moved nearer to the water's edge, shining the torch in the direction indicated by the line and holding the gaff at the ready. He could see the fish now, a fair-sized conger. I backed away and brought the fish in on a wave, in went the gaff, and Harry struggled up the slope (two steps forward and one step back) and across the shingle to the base of the cliff, dragging the conger behind him. It was a fish of about 25-pounds. I laid down the rod and killed it by slicing through the backbone behind the head before unhooking the trace.

Quickly we set up the rods again, experience having shown that the chances of catching a conger were never better than when one had just been landed. Our best spell of fishing from Durdle Door produced three fish of over 20-pounds, plus a couple of whips returned, in three-and-a-half hours. The biggest conger which we landed from this beach was just on 40-pounds. Other local beaches have produced similar fish to the same techniques.

All was still again so we poured out some more coffee. As we forced down the first mouthful, a reel clicked a couple of times causing a variety of scalds and spillages. After five minutes without further movement I reeled in to find the bait reduced to a strip of skin. We laughed about the time that Terry had had a series of such bites which he was unable to hook. Eventually, by holding his rod and striking so violently that he almost suffered injury, he managed to hook the culprit. After a brief struggle I went down the beach with the gaff but on seeing the apparition before me on the shingle I again uttered those immortal words, 'You gaff it!' *It* turned out to be a $2\frac{1}{2}$-pound squid. There was more to come. The squid was immediately cut up as bait and, ever optimistic, I put the whole head, weighing about $\frac{3}{4}$-pound, on my hook and swung it out as best I could into the deep hole close under the rocks of the Door. Some time later a fierce bite and strong run was met with a powerful strike. Nothing—the only decent fish of the night missed, probably because of the outsized bait and relatively small hook. A cruel lesson in matching bait to tackle.

We returned to reality; a few more clicks and this time there was obviously something interested. Again the other baits were retrieved, this time it was Harry's rod, and again the line went. Another strike and another fish was hooked. Five minutes later I gaffed a second conger of about 10-pounds through its lower jaw.

As Harry removed the hook, using a pair of long-nosed pliers, I pinned the eel down before returning it to the water with an exhortation to come back in a few years' time.

Over the years we have caught many conger of more than 20-pounds, both from the beach and from our small dinghy. We have never yet come across the vicious, fearsome and malevolent creatures described by some sea fishing authors. We try to play our fish out so that it is not rolling or twisting on the surface and is therefore easier to gaff. On board the dinghy they are lowered into a sack and the nylon cut above the trace, the sack is then tied up at the mouth and put under the seat. Normally, the conger does not move about very much or struggle in the dark sack. I can remember one night in particular when we had five or six conger in a large sack under the seat of the boat with a nervous visiting angler sitting over that particular seat. Occasionally there would be a coughing sound from within the sack. Every time this happened our visitor would nearly leap out of the boat. In the end Harry swapped places with him and after that there were no more problems.

The conger is a large eel often associated with rough rocky terrain. The very heavy tackle which is usually recommended for conger fishing is aimed at dealing with the conditions rather than the fish. Anyone who has tried to break a snagged line while fishing from the shore will know how difficult it is. Even a 30-pound B.S. line can be almost unbreakable unless the angler has a very firm stance or room to move. Therefore, before deciding what type of tackle to use for conger fishing one must assess the conditions. If a large conger manages to anchor itself in a hole it is almost impossible to extract it. One possibility is to use very heavy line and try to winch it out, another is to have medium or heavy line and wait until it decides to let go (you could be there for days). It will generally be much easier to employ tug-of-war tactics if it is possible to get a vertical pull on the fish, e.g. from a large boat or a ledge directly above the conger. This type of shore fishing is carried out very successfully from the rocks around the Portland area of Dorset where specimens of well over 50-pounds have been caught.

An alternative method, which we have favoured, is to fish less snaggy places close to rough ground while using lighter tackle.

The morning after: a 40-pound conger taken from the beach.

The only item of tackle which is essential to both boat and beach fishing for conger is the trace of wire, or very heavy nylon, which will withstand the abrasive action of the eel's teeth. The trace must be long enough to keep the main nylon line clear of the fish's jaws and provided that the angler has not fallen asleep or allowed the fish to gorge the bait completely, fifteen to eighteen inches between hook and swivel should be sufficient. We normally make the traces up prior to going fishing with 4/0 bronzed hooks and 30-pound B.S. nylon-covered steel wire. But if such traces are thrown into a fishing bag and left there they tend to become kinked and weakened and care must be taken that such damaged traces are not used. We have seen many good fish lost by anglers who have not checked their tackle before casting out. One thing that many years of fishing has taught us is that every knot, trace, hook and line must be tested before beginning to fish and also after hooking a snag or a fish. Carelessness could lose you that fish of a lifetime.

From both dinghy and beach, nylon lines of 18 to 30-pounds B.S. have proved equal to all that was asked of them. On one occasion a conger of 39-pounds was landed from the beach, without undue difficulty, on nylon of only 9½-pounds B.S. (I picked up the wrong spool on the way out from the house). This fish took about fifteen minutes to bring to the gaff. However, when using comparatively light tackle it is necessary to have the slipping clutch of the reel set correctly and not screwed down to its full extent. Large pike, carp and salmon are landed every day on similar tackle and, conditions permitting, conger can also be caught on such gear. We would be the last to recommend ridiculously fine lines, but some thought should be given to the conditions and circumstances of each trip in the light of what has been said.

Female conger are usually larger than the males, as the latter appear to stick at 2- or 3-feet in length. Examples of very rapid growth by congers kept in an aquarium have been quoted by Kennedy (several fish growing 10—15-pounds per year). The ear bones of a 29-pound conger which was caught at Durdle Door indicated that it was approximately twenty years of age, a much slower growth-rate than the aquarium fish. This is only to be expected in British waters because the conger does not tolerate cold winters well and will die if the water temperature falls to about 1°C. Mass deaths of conger were reported in the cold winters of 1947 and 1963. They do, however, feed well at times in the depths of winter. We have caught one off the beach on 30 December and have seen other good fish caught in January.

Finally, the loss of a conger does not necessarily mean the fish will not return. At times they can be extremely bold. On one beach fishing trip, a good fish was lost, at the gaff, by a local angler who, in true Dorset fashion, believes in hefty traces. The trace was characteristically constructed of what we could only describe as light fencing wire. Shortly afterwards a run developed on Harry's rod and after a brief struggle a 20-pound conger was landed. It was fairly hooked and there, still hanging from its jaw, was the recently lost wire trace. The modest fight that the conger put up was clearly a result of its recent struggles on the other rod.

10

Playing hard to get

THE GREY MULLET

The thick-lipped grey mullet, like the bass, is essentially a surface-swimming fish which spends a large proportion of its time in shallow inshore waters. Both species are excellent in terms of sport and as food fish but there the resemblance ends. As already mentioned, this species, which is much the most common British mullet, had been found comparatively easy to catch up to weights of a couple of pounds.

We had fished for mullet from the quays and piers, such as those at Poole and Weymouth, by using fairly light tackle, often described as 'freshwater tackle' and baiting with bread in various forms (flake, crust and paste) or with small ragworms.

Even in those early days, we were aware, by way of the angling press and by word of mouth from other anglers, that larger mullet were sometimes caught, apparently on tackle similar to ours, by 'those in the know' who fished from the open shore. It was said that heavy groundbaiting and float fishing with maggot bait was successful in rocky areas such as Durlston Bay, near Swanage.

During our bass fishing trips we would often see mullet in large numbers, sometimes far greater than those of the bass which we caught. Many a time, as we made our way back to the carpark after an evening's bass fishing, one of us would say something like, 'Just think of the sport we could have, if only we had a good method for catching the mullet.'

For two or three years we were so absorbed in trying to catch bass that the mullet were more or less ignored. Occasionally, during a quiet spell, we would spin through huge shoals of mullet more in hope than in expectation, but it was only rarely that a mullet would be taken, sometimes foul-hooked. The hooks were generally found to be lodged in the base of the pelvic fins

94

but occasionally the tail treble of a Mepps Mino or even of a large plug would be well inside the mouth, a position which it could only have attained by means of a fish trying to take the lure. The fish caught in this way, by accident so to speak, ranged in size from 8-ounces to almost 4-pounds, but little satisfaction was to be extracted from landing them.

The useful tips gained from this 'chuck and chance it' approach were, firstly, that the mullet had definite *preferred* regions of the shore along which they tended to congregate. These regions differed from time to time, particularly in relation to weather conditions, but almost always the greatest concentrations of fish were to be found in those spots where large amounts of debris accumulated at the high water mark. Secondly, mullet were easy to see, because they often lay at the water surface, or a few inches below it. Ripples, boils, swirls, backs, fins or noses almost invariably gave away their presence. Our eyes became attuned to distinguishing the swirl of a mullet from the disturbance caused by the swell passing over a submerged rock. The glint of a silver-grey flank beneath the breaking waves would often reveal a shoal feeding on sea-bed algae, or a pyramid of snout adorned with plump, pink-flushed lips could be picked out amongst the little triangular wavelets caused by a squall of wind.

It soon became possible to distinguish between signs of bass and those of mullet. The upper lobe of the tail fin, which is often the most conspicuous feature of both species, is sharply peaked in the mullet and somewhat rounded in the bass. The mouth of a bass is, of course, rather larger than that of a mullet; it is also somewhat paler when it gapes open. Given a glimpse of a head (a much more frequent event than one might suppose), that of the bass creates the impression of having a circular, black-bruised area surrounding the eye.

The small number of mullet which we had caught fought quite differently, with less acceleration and fewer fast runs, than similar sized bass. The take of the mullet was of course, less fierce but these fish were by far the most dogged fighters and almost invariably struggled all the way to the net, even after five or more minutes play on an 8- or 10-pound line.

Lastly, the oft repeated myth of the *soft mouthed* mullet was brought into perspective. The lips of these fish are tough and rubbery resembling, as much as anything, those of a chub. Fish which came off the hook in the course of the fight frequently left one or two massive squarish scales on the points of the treble hooks, indicating that they had been foul hooked in their armour plating. A hook once firmly fixed in the mouth of a mullet can be the very devil to remove and, more than once, has even required surgery.

These then were our first encounters with grey mullet on the open shore, and they were sufficient to arouse considerable interest in the possibility of catching these fishy enigmas. Almost all the mullet which we had caught in these situations, when they were subjected to the statutory post mortem, were found to contain only the maggots of the seaweed fly, often hundreds in a single fish. If the water was dirty with silt, the thin-walled part of the stomach, similar to the crop of a bird, contained maggots. The other stomach chamber, rather like a muscular gizzard, would be packed with fine, gritty sediment. The two items were always perfectly separated. A little research at this stage revealed that the thick-lipped mullet and many of its relatives are basically adapted to feeding on fine particles.

With regard to their feeding habits, as mentioned already, they are generally, and correctly, supposed to feed on filaments of algae and on the microscopic plant and animal material which is associated with this algae. The mullet's herbivorous inclinations are confirmed by the enormously long gut, which is only too obvious to one trying to clean these fish in the traditional manner by slitting open the belly. In fact, many other species of fish which feed on algae have fairly short guts, and their digestive processes are assisted by the presence of a very strong acid secreted in the stomach. Mullet, in contrast, have neutral or alkaline stomach secretions and rely on the specialised 'gizzard' or *colloid mill* which, with the aid of swallowed sediment to act as a grinding paste, smashes up the swallowed cells.

Another interesting fact about the feeding of grey mullets relates to their ability to select, or sort out, fine particles of a narrow size-range, from sediment which they suck into the mouth. This selection is achieved by a sophisticated filtering apparatus in the throat. Young (small) grey mullets feed on the same sort of detritus, algae and small animals as do their older

Unhooking a 5-pound, fly-caught mullet.

relatives. Studies on striped mullet off the coast of Florida have shown that the fish feed almost entirely in the hours of daylight, with a peak of activity just before midday. Similar information is not available for British mullets but they are certainly active daytime feeders.

Like bass, thick-lipped mullet are fairly slow-growing fish. Their age can best be determined by reading the scales which have very clear growth lines. Mullet only mature at nine to eleven years of age when they are about 14- to 18-inches in length, so many immature mullet must be killed each year by anglers and commercial fishermen alike. A good specimen of about 5-pounds weight would probably be not far short of twenty years of age.

The way of life of grey mullets is obviously a successful one because a great many species are very abundant and they are distributed throughout the world. In Hawaii, young striped mullet stay in the very shallow water of estuaries and intertidal pools, only moving offshore when they reach about 2-inches in length. On the coast of Dorset, shoals of tiny mullet swim in the

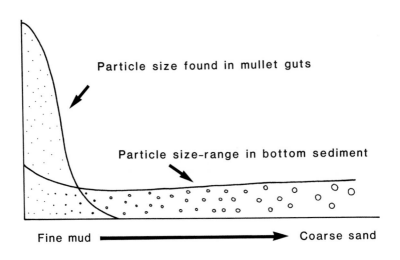

Particle size found in mullet guts

Particle size-range in bottom sediment

Fine mud ➜ Coarse sand

38. Selection of fine particles by American grey mullet. Fine mud has the greatest food value.

intertidal rock pools, rippling the surface and leaving V-shaped wakes just like miniatures of those made by the adults on estuary mudflats. When disturbed, the small mullet disappear as if by magic and may then be found wedged into tiny rock crevices and under stones.

To return now to the business of fishing for mullet. We had managed to catch a few fish by spinning, therefore in 1972, plans were made for a serious attempt to take greater numbers of fish. At first, a traditional approach using float-fished bread produced a few infrequent bites and even less fish. Whilst fishing in this way we would watch, with some frustration, the shoals of mullet feeding within five or six feet of our boots. It was quite apparent that, in most cases, these fish were not feeding beneath the surface but actually right in the surface film. It was also obvious that the fish had no interest in bread or any natural detritus but were

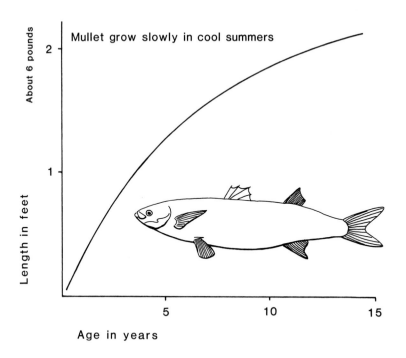

39.   Growth of the thick-lipped grey mullet (aged by scale rings).

feeding exclusively on the larvae or pupae of the seaweed flies, which were being washed out of the weed by the incoming tide.

The first real glimmer of success came to the rod of Fred Philpott. Fred was a student from Brunel University who spent a year working with us down in Wareham. He was a lanky, long-haired young man with a pleasant manner and a ready smile, and above all he was, like the rest of us, a fanatical angler. An experienced beach caster, with many good catches of sole and other flatfish to his name, Fred took to bass spinning like a duck to water. His interest was consolidated in the early summer of his stay when, on an evening trip with Terry, he landed three bass on a borrowed plastic plug. The fish in question weighed 5-, 6½- and 9-pounds, but Fred was not satisfied. Like the rest of us he was fascinated by the tantalising sight of all those mullet.

The following evening found Fred alone, getting out of his car and putting up an 11-foot match rod with a small fixed spool reel (an old Intrepid) loaded with 4-pound line. Leaving the spinning rod in the car to avoid temptation, he set off on the two-mile walk to the scene of his previous night's success. The sea was calm with only a light south-westerly breeze and Fred made good time along the narrow undercliff path. The spring tide was two-thirds of the way in. Full of anticipation, he waded through the shallow water past Black Ledge, knowing that he would be cut off for at least a couple of hours either side of high water.

Half-a-mile further along the beach, as he approached the appointed place, there was a strong smell of decaying kelp and his boots squelched through mounds of well-rotted weed. The little embayment in the cliff was reasonably well sheltered from anywhere but the south and south-west. Waves from these 'quarters' were reflected back from the cliff and the resultant confusion of swells dumped every fragment of flotsam, jetsam and weed onto the high water mark at this point.

There they were in the dirty brown water—mullet of all sizes; possibly sixty or seventy fish were concentrated into an area not much bigger than a snooker table. Fred tied on a size 12 eyed-hook and baited it with a cube of crust. By holding the long rod almost vertical, the light breeze eddying from the cliff was just sufficient to billow out the fine line, enabling him to drop the cube of crust in the midst of the shoal. At the first attempt the bread was taken by a good mullet, sipped in more delicately than one might suppose for such a large fish. A sharp lift of the rod tip by the somewhat surprised Fred was met with only the merest resistance as the hook came away, having just nicked the lip of the mullet. There was no doubt that the fish had felt it though. With an enormous boiling of the surface the entire shoal dispersed in an instant.

It was almost fifteen minutes before the fish reassembled and it was again possible for him to drift his bait amongst them. The crust was dapped in the middle of a group of churning mullet once more. Three or four times his bait was brushed off the hook by the back or tail of a fish passing nearby. He baited up and cast again, and a small fish turned towards the bait. Holding his breath, wrist muscles tense with anticipation, Fred waited. The cube of crust was drawn into an open mouth. This time the strike connected firmly and the fish, seemingly confused, allowed itself to be drawn shorewards with only a gentle flapping of its body. It touched the rim of the waiting landing net and suddenly became aware of its plight, tearing away in a series of strong three or four-yard runs. Soon the fish was fifteen yards out from the sea's edge and the line was draped in bits of weed like a string of little signal flags. It was two or three minutes later before the mullet was enveloped in the net and slid from the sea.

It was a 2½-pounder, quite a good fish by *our* usual quayside standards. The hook was removed and the fish returned to the water. An hour later Fred packed it in and made his way back along the beach, having landed one other 1½-pound fish. His modest catch was one of several that we had made on bread crust, but was significant in the fact that the fish had been taken while they were feeding in the surface film.

No doubt the reader is already way ahead of us and wondering why we had not tried fly fishing. Truth to tell, we had already discussed this possibility but Harry and I lacked the confidence to use a dry fly in the sea.

In fact, the first attempt at using a fly was made by Rick, a keen trout fisherman with no experience of sea fishing at all. It was our persuasive tales of huge fish and vivid descriptions of the 'mother and father of all evening rises' that did the trick. The analogy, if memory serves right, was that of a trout farm at feeding time. What trout angler could resist?—certainly not Rick.

The outcome of it all was that Rick and I made an evening trip down to the sea. The sun was already low over the western cliffs of the bay as I, carrying my faithful old spinning rod, and Rick with a light 8-foot trout fly rod, no. 6 line and 4-pound B.S. cast, walked the fifty yards from the carpark to the sea. The sight which met our eyes scarcely lived up to our earlier descriptions. About a dozen mullet were ensconced in 'carpark corner'; slowly they cruised about, turning and turning again, each with about half-an-inch of snout projecting above the surface film as they mopped up maggots floating on the water.

The sea was dark and waves of about a foot in height were breaking amongst the boulders. Rick sat back on a big rock and took out his fly box. I walked ten yards along to the left of the feeding fish and began to cast my plug. Rick selected a dry Coachman, much as he might have done had he been about to fish the evening rise on one of the local chalk streams. With obvious trepidation he walked to where the breaking waves were splashing over his rubber-booted feet. He worked out about ten yards of line before allowing the fly to settle on the water. For half-an-hour he fished, trying everything he could think of. The fly was allowed to sit on the surface, vibrated, skated back and even drowned, all to no avail until, suddenly, it disappeared and a fish was on. The resulting plunge of the hooked fish was so powerful that the cast could not take the shock and parted with a sharp crack.

Stunned, Rick sat down to tie on another fly and as is my wont, I gave vent to a few choice words about the fish's parentage. The dry Coachman had been the only fly of its kind in the box, so a small Olive nondescript of about the same size was tied on to the remainder of the cast. It was now becoming quite dark and we were just discussing whether to 'give them best' when a firm pull on Rick's fly line was met by an adept lift of the rod. This time the fish was well hooked and line buzzed from the reel as it moved off in a series of strong runs which, as we now know, often characterise the fight of a mullet taken under these conditions. Gradually the lost line was regained and the fish came closer to where I waited with the net. Even in the dim light we could see that it was a good mullet of about 4-pounds hooked in the mouth. Just as Rick was manipulating the fish into the net and heaving sighs of relief it made a final desperate plunge and the hook hold gave way. The feeling was rather like finding two pence and losing a ten pound note. We were both pleased to have seen a fish hooked on fly but its ultimate loss was a tragedy.

The following morning a gale blew up and the strong winds continued throughout that series of tides. Two weeks later when conditions were again suitable for fishing, a bright, calm Sunday afternoon saw the old contemptibles, Terry, Harry and I, venturing down to the coast again. We were intent on going to 'Casey's ledge', a sheltered corner where there was almost invariably a good accumulation of seaweed. Once again it was a spring tide, high water would be at about eight o'clock in the evening and we were prepared to stay until dark.

Each of us was equipped with a fly rod and reel of some sort. Terry's was a fine built-cane rod which had seen much service with the trout of Lake Windermere. I also had a built-cane rod, but it was now six inches shorter than its original 9ft 6in. following some hamfisted fly fishing experiments on the banks of the River Tyne. Harry had a cheap, hollow glass rod purchased expressly for the occasion. I had, fortuitously as it turned out, brought a few white maggots left over from the previous week's dace fishing. As we tackled up there was no sign of any fish at all, the tide was still two yards from the edge of the deposited seaweed. A scrape of the welly boot soon revealed that the weed pile was in an advanced state of breakdown; internally, it was hot, steaming and seething with seaweed fly maggots.

By now we had begun to 'get the message' about these mullet. The rising tide was obviously likely to wash maggots from their hiding places and as they drifted onto the surface of the sea the mullet, quick on the uptake, were accustomed to make hay while the sun shone.

Harry and I sat down on a couple of handy boulders to await the anticipated arrival of the fish but Terry, a much more experienced fly fisherman, tied on a 2½-inch, Waddington pattern, blue and silver salmon fly, armed with a size ten treble, to try for a bass. As we watched, he cast well out over the clear water and stripped the line back into his left hand in a neat figure of eight. Obviously there were not many bass about, for it was difficult to imagine how any fish could ignore such an attractively presented lure.

The tide was now beginning to lap at the base of the weed and little creamy-white patches of maggots were floating off as the water level rose between the big grey boulders. A few feet from the water's edge we noticed one or two swirls, almost like small dace rising. The mullet were approaching closer as they swam up current towards our position.

All three of us were standing up and casting now. Terry fished on with his streamer fly but Harry and I had attached small, light-coloured dry flies in the hope that they would resemble drifting maggots. Quite a few fish were feeding actively in front of us and many were well within casting range. The minutes ticked by without a take except for a tiny bass which impaled itself on the salmon fly. It was obvious that the fish could see the little dry flies from the fact that they would swim up to them and then turn emphatically to one side to avoid them.

Terry was into another fish by now and this was clearly a better one. Already the fly line was down to the backing and there was little sign of the fish stopping. Harry and I reeled in, laid the rods down and went to his aid. Harry picked up the large carp net and stood ready. 'It'll be a bit yet,' muttered Terry, as his adversary took back all the line which he had just recovered. The fish ran fast and hard, shearing and kiting across the tide so that we had to hurry along the beach to keep in touch. 'Must be a nice bass,' said Terry. 'Perhaps it's a small one foul hooked,' I retorted, a remark greeted with the disdain it deserved.

At last the fish was tiring and now we could see glimpses of a spiky fin as it twisted and turned ten yards out. Another couple of minutes and it was drawn over Harry's waiting net—a fine bass of $6\frac{3}{4}$-pounds; a grand fish for a trout fly rod and 8-pound cast.

We all returned to our fishing. The mullet were more numerous now. Small tight groups of a dozen or so fish were almost falling over one another to gulp down the thousands of drifting maggots. I shouted to Harry, 'I'm going to prog a couple of maggots on my fly.' 'Worth a try,' came the reply. Feverishly I reeled in, and thinking about the shortcomings of my casting technique, threaded four maggots onto the bend of the fly hook. I recast and the fly landed squarely in the middle of a group of feeding mullet. The pull, when it came, took me completely by surprise and I forgot to strike. Two more casts and nothing happened so I reeled in and examined the fly. The maggots were flat and dead, like little bits of translucent yellow plastic, but the skins appeared to be undamaged. The sea water had killed and dehydrated them, so I put on some fresh ones and flicked them out again. This time I was ready when the line twitched along the water surface. A sharp strike resulted in a well-hooked 3-pound mullet. Harry had got the message by this time and was already baiting his fly with some of the maggots. I played and landed my own mullet and as I turned back towards the sea the rods of my companions were well bent. Both the fish were mullet, Terry's 3½-pounds and Harry's nearly ½-pound heavier. The bites came infrequently to Harry and I now, but at intervals of about ten or fifteen minutes, Terry hooked a succession of bass on his streamer fly, none as good as his second, but several of between 4- and 6-pounds each.

As dusk fell the tide was half-way out and only a few fish were now visible. We picked up our tackle and put the eight larger fish which we had kept into the obligatory fertiliser sack. On the way back we discussed the fishing. The salmon fly had seemed to be quite an effective way of taking bass under the prevailing conditions. Harry and I had finished up by taking a couple of mullet each but after a while our dry flies had ceased to float. The fish had shown little or no interest in a sunken fly, whether adorned with maggots or not. Live, wriggling maggots seemed to induce bites with almost alarming speed so long as they remained on the surface. The fish had been swimming with their eyes just in the surface film and obviously were well able to see both the natural maggots and the anglers' flies and to distinguish between the living article and the inanimate feather imitation.

Many of the observations we had made in previous years were now beginning to fall into place. Some of the reasons why mullet and bass congregated at certain spots and times were now obvious. Places where weed accumulates in periods of rough weather are where seaweed flies collect to breed. Some of these sites are easily identified in a single walk along the shore at any time of day, although the weather and particularly the wind strength and direction are likely to favour specific places at different times. In other words, one place may be better than another, according to conditions. The second vital consideration is the state of the tide; under calm sea conditions, the seaweed fly larvae are only available to the fish at the top of the biggest spring tides. Rough weather in which waves reach further up the beach can easily extend the period worth fishing to seven or eight days in each series of tides. Against this, rough conditions can make it tricky, to say the least, to fish with a fly.

One of the substances most frequently cast up on beaches is expanded polystyrene. This white, fluffy, incredibly light material in the form of cups and blocks of packing material is washed and blown up on every shore in the country. The natural progression in dry fly fishing for mullet, in view of our problems with 'drowned' flies, was to make permanent floaters. At first we simply picked up a few granules of polystyrene from a handy piece of flotsam and threaded them up the hook shank. A bunch of ordinary, commercially produced maggots was placed on the bend. The numbers of mullet taken on fly leapt sharply on the introduction of this refinement. The foam was, in fact, a bit of a nuisance and was easily flicked off the hook during casting or, on occasions, it slid over the eye of the hook and up the cast.

Polystyrene on the hook is clearly just a newer version of a very old idea, for 'cork maggots' were used in freshwater fishing many years ago. It is only a short step from fragments of polystyrene to the use of modern polyethylene foam, which is much tougher and more durable than polystyrene. With a minimum of whipping at either end, a neat and permanently floating 'maggot fly' can be created.

Ideally, the maggot fly would be used without the adornment of real maggots, which soon die when exposed to salt water. Experience has shown however that, just as the mullet had avoided our original dry flies, they are perfectly capable of distinguishing a polyethylene maggot, however realistic, from the genuine article. The ability of the fish to discern small objects is verified in other ways. The finest cast which it is practicable to use (5 to 6-pounds B.S.) is easily visible to the surface-feeding fish. Frequently they will cruise towards a cast lying on the surface and submerge within a few inches of it, only to resurface on the other side. Even a fly line false cast well above the heads of feeding fish will often be greeted by a violent flourish of activity as they disperse. To obtain the best results it is necessary not just to bait the fly with maggots, but to replace the maggots every half-dozen casts or after every missed bite. Similarly, mullet are easily frightened by the presence of an angler on the shore, melting away like magic should the angler disturb them in any way by a sudden movement, or even by his shadow falling on the water.

The original hooks used ranged from size fourteen to about size six eyed and bronzed fly hooks. As in most, if not all, angling, only the best quality hooks are worth bothering with. The hooks on which commercially prepared flies are tied are often much too brittle and if they touch one of the cementstone boulders on the back cast the resultant loss of hook point will often only be noticed after an abortive strike. Worse still, the hook may break in a fish with disastrous results. Fine wire hooks are equally unsuitable because they are liable to turn a point on touching a rock.

The main hazards of fly fishing from the sea shore are rough weather and weed. Loose weed, which is the key to the presence of bass and mullet shoals, will frequently drape itself over even a high floating plastic fly line. The result of this entanglement can be extremely frustrating, particularly when it is combined with a moderate surf. In no time at all it seems, the line is buried under several pounds of floating kelp and, in trying to sort out the resulting mess, a broken cast is the usual result. Worse still, five minutes of valuable fishing time is thus lost. When this little scenario occurs for the fifth time in succession tempers are apt to become somewhat frayed.

Frequently, before the mullet concentrate at high water, it is profitable to fish six inches below the surface using light float tackle and a size twelve hook baited with maggots. In this way the period of sport can be prolonged considerably. The fish thus taken on the float will usually be considerably smaller—say 1-pound—compared with an average $2\frac{1}{2}$-pounder taken on the surface fly. Many good mullet have been caught by fly fishing. The best single bag was five fish with a total weight of over 25-pounds, taken by Terry in one evening. A catch of this size together with the usual quota of missed bites, lost fish and smaller fish returned, represents quite a hectic spell of fishing. In such circumstances it is not unusual to feel that the entire trip has been spent playing, landing and losing fish.

On the maggot fly, mullet of over 4-pounds are not out of the ordinary, and fish of over 5-pounds are caught quite frequently. To add to the excitement there is always the chance of a good bass for variety because bass, of all sizes, join the mullet at their feast. On one occasion we were joined by Robin, an enthusiastic and successful fly fisherman, intent on trying his hand at catching a mullet. Predictably, at the first visible signs of moving fish, he decided to have a go, leaving the rest of us to go on to one of our favourite spots. He did not follow us as expected and when we returned carrying a couple of nice mullet, we found Robin still fishing in the same place. Behind him on the rocks lay bass of $7\frac{1}{2}$-, 6-, and $5\frac{1}{2}$-pounds. All had taken a maggot fly which he had cast to individual, 'rising' fish. Needless to say he was impressed with the sport and the rest of us were envious of his catch.

To take good mullet on fly tackle *consistently* needs a certain amount of practice. Bites may be detected in different ways. Some of us prefer to use relatively large maggot flies on hooks of about size eight, so that the mullet can be seen actually taking them into their mouths. Others watch for the line to *draw* across the surface. Either of these methods can be very effective, particularly given good eyesight and calm conditions. For those (like me) with eyesight which is less acute, a third approach is possible and probably more fish have been taken in this way than any other. The cast is aimed to place the fly beyond a group of feeding mullet; after a couple of seconds the rod is raised very slowly and the weight of the bow in the fly line allowed to draw the fly through the shoal. If the fish are feeding well, and have not been scared by the cast, a *take* may come at any instant and can be detected by a change in the movement of the line which, as the rod is raised, slides smoothly back towards the angler. The line may slow down or stop or the bow may straighten perceptibly. Sometimes there will even be a knock or pull on the rod tip, but this usually indicates that a fish has brushed the line with its dorsal fin or bumped into the cast with its open mouth. Many of the abortive strikes, at what seem to be good bites, are due to these causes. Striking at fish which have bumped into the cast in their feeding frenzy will sometimes result in them being

Five mullet caught on the maggot fly. The average weight of the fish is 5-pounds.

hooked on the outside of the lips or in the nostril.

Having struck a mullet successfully it is usually worth taking a couple of backward paces to ensure a tight line. This may be more difficult than it sounds if the angler is standing on a rock surrounded by water or if he has surmounted a pile of decomposing slippery seaweed. In view of these hazards, the most conspicuous characteristics of our mullet fishermen are their soaking wet clothing and their distinctive smell.

Once it is hooked the mullet will usually do one of two things. At times a fish will simply jag slowly on the line and allow itself to be led to the net. If it can be netted without realising its danger, the fight will be over in a minute or less. If on the other hand the mullet takes fright, either on seeing the net or the angler or, more usually, on being hooked, it will normally make a series of powerful pacy runs. The total amount of line taken is normally

109

more or less proportional to the size of the fish. A large mullet of 5- to 6-pounds will take a full fly line and ten yards of backing off the reel without much trouble. A fish which, when hooked, accelerates quickly to a high speed and keeps going is either a bass or a mullet which has been foul-hooked. The latter soon becomes obvious by the way in which the hooked fish is inclined to shear across to left or right.

As in spinning, fish which escape after a few minutes are often found to have been foul-hooked in a scale. If possible, fish should be played along the shore away from the feeding shoal. A through action rod and a smooth check on the fly reel are important in avoiding broken casts. As in playing any powerful fish on comparatively light tackle and small hooks the important thing is to be patient, to take one's time and, above all, to try and anticipate the movements of the fish. Mullet should always be netted, for more fish are lost in vain attempts to beach them than in any other way. Even the best hold of a size twelve hook will not stand the full force of the last desperate lunge of a big mullet.

A gaff is not a good idea for two reasons; firstly, a large mullet scale may shield the point of the sharpest gaff and, secondly, the gaff is quite likely to penetrate the body cavity of the fish, the contents of which may then contaminate and taint the flesh.

If possible a quick survey should be made to determine the probable places where mullet will turn up on forthcoming spring tides. On the actual fishing trip one may be confronted with a variety of conditions. If it is calm and mullet are rather thin on the ground with, perhaps, a fish showing only every few yards, it is debatable whether fly fishing is worth while. Casting to individual fish is a possibility and will sometimes result in a good fish taking the fly, but often it will simply be an object lesson in the difficulty of deceiving the humble mullet when it has plenty of time to cast its eagle eye over the fly line, cast and fly. It may well be more profitable to put up the spinning rod, tie on a floating plug, and spin for bass for an hour or so in the hope of the mullet aggregating into feeding groups. The third alternative is a brisk walk along the beach in an attempt to find more intense concentrations of fish. Float fishing can also be productive under these circumstances.

It is sometimes possible to *create* actively feeding groups of fish

by ground-baiting or feeding with weed and the maggots of the
seaweed fly. This is no job for the squeamish, as it is best achieved
by manhandling the stinking, steaming, glutinous, brown weed
into the sea where it will gradually be dispersed by the rising tide
and breaking waves.

On another day there may be a moderate breeze and mullet
could be feeding ravenously in small restricted areas. In these
circumstances the fish are sometimes difficult to scare. This may
also be the case when the approaching dusk helps to conceal the
angler from the fish. The main problem with actively feeding fish
is getting a fly into the shoal, for frequently such groups of mullet
will be found within a foot of the water's edge, right in the
breaking waves. It then becomes necessary to cast parallel to the
beach, from upwind if possible, flicking a loop of line out to sea
as the cast is made, so as to try and avoid the fly line being cast
ashore amongst the piles of weed.

Less easy to deal with, or to accept, is the situation when
maggots or casters (pupae) of the flies have been driven out from
the shore by the joint actions of the wind and undertow. This
results in the need for long casting, and it reaches a point at which
the difficulties of fishing dictate that the angler resorts to spinning
or fishing with a float at long range.

A strong, longshore current may concentrate a band of feeding
fish close to regions where the cliff or rock ledges push out into
the sea. The mullet will then be visible close in to the shore,
stemming the tide, facing the current and simply filtering the
surface-drifting maggots carried to them by the flow. Such fish
may be fairly easy to catch by casting the fly uptide and allowing
it to drift down to them. These conditions normally result in a
higher proportion of fish hooked on the outside of the lips than
usual. This is due to the drifting cast contacting the mouths and
snouts of feeding mullet.

As the summer wears on into September and October, fish are
still to be found feeding on seaweed fly maggots, but rough sea
conditions and dirty water are more frequent. Sand smelts, little
mullet-like fish which ring the surface like large minnows,
become a significant feature close inshore. It is under these
conditions that a spinner, a plug or, best of all, a streamer fly, will
take mullet. Bass will also show at the surface under these

conditions as they zig-zag in their hunt for small bait-fishes.

Masses of seaweed lying on the high water mark will generally behave like a garden compost heap. The decaying contents of the heap generate a great deal of heat even in the colder months of the year. In fact the air temperature has very little effect on the development of a 'good brew' of weed and maggots, and the latter can be found at almost any season. Very hot, dry weather, although it is generally favourable to the presence and feeding activity of the fish, can quickly dry up even large quantities of 'maggot food'. Prolonged hot spells, such as the summer of 1976, may make fly fishing almost useless by destroying the main source of attraction.

In contrast, when the weather is very wet, mud will be washed into the sea and any sort of fishing may be difficult. In an effort to induce bites under these conditions it was felt that some sort of vibrating lure was needed which the fish could detect by sensing the movement. It is well known that anglers fishing for grey mullet in Christchurch Harbour use small Mepps spinners with some success. We were already aware, however, that normal Mepps with heavy metal bodies were liable to snag the bottom unless they were retrieved very quickly. To enable a slow retrieve the metal bodies of the spoons were replaced by streamlined, balsa wood 'torpedoes'. These wooden bodies were painted white to enchance visibility in murky water conditions and even though they were given limited trials they proved attractive to both bass and mullet. The principle of using a buoyant body and a bar spoon would seem to have considerable potential in other types of angling. Unweighted, they would allow a slow retrieve over heavy weed for pike fishing. Behind a suitable lead they could well be as effective as wooden or plastic Devon minnows for salmon fishing. The scope would seem to be large.

A couple of tips are worth noting with regard to preparing fish for the table. Mullet must be scaled before they can be filleted. If this is done at home the huge scales get everywhere, so it is a good practise to scale the fish while it is still wet, and before leaving the beach at the end of a session. No knife is necessary to scale a mullet; if the fingertips are carefully run under the scales from the tail towards the head the entire flank can be cleared in a single movement. A word of warning at this point: the angler should, in handling either bass or mullet, take care to avoid running the very sharp fin spines into the finger ends. Accidents of this kind are liable to result in days or even weeks of discomfort. Large fish can be filleted easily with very little waste; smaller fish should be gutted as soon as possible. It is not absolutely necessary to gut either species because the fillets can be removed easily from whole fish. Both bass and mullet make superb eating and are similar in flavour. Wash and dry the fillets, place them under a medium grill, season with salt, pepper, butter and a squeeze of lemon. Cook for ten to fifteen minutes (according to thickness), turning a couple of times. With a slice of bread and butter or a few chips they are a gourmet's dream.

In conclusion we will add a cautionary word about fishing close under the face of crumbling cliffs. Apart from the risk of being buried by a cliff fall there is always a danger of being hit on the head by a pebble descending from a great height. On no account should one dig or otherwise disturb the base of such unstable cliffs. Landslips are most frequent when heavy rain follows a spell of hot dry weather and at these times it is wise to wear a hard hat if it is necessary to stand in the danger area.

Anyone who spends a lot of fishing time on Dorset beaches is likely, at some time, to experience near misses from the crumbling shale. On one occasion Harry, Terry, Fred and I were strung out along a straight stretch of beach assiduously spinning and fly fishing for scattered shoals of bass and mullet. Every few minutes pebbles would rattle down from above and all four were keeping half-an-eye open for nearby falls. Suddenly a rumbling sound was heard from the vicinity of Fred's position. The attention of the rest of us was immediately focused on the point. Clouds of grey dust billowed out to sea obscuring the entire beach and as the dust cleared, a huge pile of freshly fallen slabs, some bigger than tea chests, was visible where Fred had been. 'My God!' said Harry, 'He's gone.' As we made our way along the rocks towards the spot, Fred's head appeared from beneath the waves and he emerged from the sea coughing and spluttering, still hanging on to his rod. On hearing the cliff rumble down behind him, he had wisely decided that discretion was the better part of valour. Without waiting, he had jumped straight out to sea only to fall forward and disappear under five feet of water.

11

'On your marks!'

SMALL-EYED RAYS AND BLACK BREAM

There is an irresistible urge to fish in waters beyond those fished by one's fellow anglers. That such a feeling is deep-rooted is evident from the manner in which the less experienced followers of the gentle art will congregate at the outer end of a long pier. Touched by the same urge it was not long before we were exploring the waters of Swanage Bay from hired rowing dinghies. At first we would hire a boat for an hour or so in the afternoon, and explore by trolling spoons and spinners as we rowed out into the bay. Of necessity we were restricted to the holiday period, the only time when boats were for hire.

In the early summer, small pollack of up to $1\frac{1}{2}$-pounds were good sport on light line and a Toby spoon. Later in the year, mackerel and garfish were the usual product of similar excursions. As we came to know the boat-hirers better we were permitted to spend an evening in the bay, and when we returned, to put the boat away by ourselves. This increase in fishing time led to attempts at bottom fishing, using worm or strips of mackerel and garfish as bait. The product of these efforts was little different to what we had experienced in using similar methods from the adjacent beaches or from the local pier.

Modest flounders, plaice and wrasse took the worms in the hours of daylight and at dusk pouting and poor cod took anything. One evening, as we returned particularly late from one of our evening trips, some members of the local angling club were just unloading their motor boat and laying out the catch on an old fish box. A couple of conger of 10- or 12-pounds each, three or four black bream of round about 1-pound, a big edible crab and, wonder of wonders, a 9-pound ray. The latter was, in

our eyes, a superb creature. In the light of our torch its pinky
grey skin gleamed dully and we could see an attractive pattern of
white undulating stripes parallel to the margin of the disc. We
talked about the fish all the way home and the following
morning we looked up the ray in Kennedy's *Sea Angler's Fishes*.
There it was, large as life, the painted or small-eyed ray, a species
of local distribution which had been caught on rod and line to a
weight of just under 11-pounds. A 9-pounder was obviously a
large fish.

Already we had put in a fair number of hours fishing without
so much as a sniff from a skate or ray. Either we were using the
wrong baits or fishing in the wrong places. The tackles
recommended by the pundits for such fish left little scope for
imagination or variation. The use of a simple running leger, with
the bait hard on or very close to the sea bed was near enough to
our usual style to make us confident, at least in this respect. Fresh
mackerel was generally quoted as a good all-round bait so we
concluded that we must be fishing in the wrong places.

The sea bed in the bay seemed to us to consist of extensive
stretches of sand and was very uniform in depth. The first thing
we needed was a decent map or chart. We bought the largest
admiralty chart available and spent some time poring over it. It
confirmed our observations; a more or less level sandy bed with
very few of the features beloved of angling authors. There were
no pinnacles, gulleys or holes within range of our small rowing
dinghy. In fact there was only one feature: running out obliquely
from the shore was a rocky ledge which seemed to extend well
out into the bay—certainly as far out as we would want to
venture. It would have to suffice. Then we came to the
problem—how did one locate such sea bed features in several
square miles of water? There were plenty of shore marks but they
were not shown on the chart and we had no refinements such as
echo sounders or Decca navigators. We watched, with more than
a passing interest, the marks used by local anglers and crabbers
but it was soon obvious that their positioning was usually
approximate within pretty wide limits. There were, nonetheless, a
couple of areas which seemed to be favoured and both were in
the general vicinity of the presumed ledge. We set out to find and
hopefully to map the ledge, using a handline tied to a 5-pound

lead. Choosing a calm sunny afternoon we traversed back and forth. There was nothing subtle about our methods and we soon realised that it was not possible to draw any sort of map but we did manage to obtain marks on a couple of features, standing five to ten feet from the surrounding sea bed in thirty feet of water. We presumed that these were sections of the ledge and we set out to fish these places regularly under a range of tidal and weather conditions.

The problem lay in the expense of the hired boat. We were forced to fish only about once in every couple of weeks and it was obviously going to take some little time to build up any sort of picture at that rate. On the first couple of trips which we made to the 'ledge mark' the efforts paid off. The first time out we boated two conger, one of 8-pounds and one of 12-pounds. Both took mackerel fillets presented on 30-pound B.S. wire traces and 4/0 hooks, the same sort of tackle which we were accustomed to use when conger fishing from the beach.

Harry and I took a second trip on a perfect evening following a hot July day. As we launched the clinker-built, varnished dinghy with a large number 12 painted on the bow, the day's sea breeze was already dying away. The usual Tobys were trolled on the way out to the mark but we had no bites; it was high tide now and there was little water movement.

The large stone which served as an anchor was lowered to the sea bed when we were still a few oar strokes from the mark. As the boat came to rest we checked that the left-hand chimney of the house on the cliff was in line with the folly on the hill and that the big elm tree was just behind the right-hand edge of the large white house. I unclipped the Toby from my line and replaced it with a 1-ounce pirk which I lowered to the sea bed and proceeded to jig up and down.

Harry rigged a simple paternoster bearing a size-six hook baited with ragworm and lowered it gently until he felt the $\frac{1}{2}$-ounce bomb tap the bottom. For half an hour neither method produced any form of action. Eventually Harry's rod tip twitched gently and he became alert; another twitch was followed by a sharp strike. 'Missed!' he exclaimed and reeled in to examine the bait. Where the worm had been threaded hung a plump black goby of about 5-inches in length. 'Let's give it a try as bait, I'll cut it in two,' I said. 'Don't bother, it's not worth it. Put it on whole and I'll try to catch another,' was the response. I killed the goby and liphooked it firmly on the 4/0 hook. A 1-ounce lead was fixed to the sliding link and the tackle was lowered slowly to the sea bed. Ten minutes later Harry reeled in another goby. His second rod, a ridiculous 5-foot glass wand with the Ambassadeur 5000 on the butt was set up in a similar manner to my own.

The sun was by now going down over the hills to the west of the bay and the street lamps along the sea front were casting rippling yellow patterns across the surface of the darkening sea. Harry began to catch a series of small pouting on the worms, so I took off the pirk and rigged up a second wire trace baited with half a pouting (liphooked head and 'shoulders'). Having caught half-a-dozen 'baits' Harry also changed to a big bait, using the other half of the pouting.

We settled down for a wait and a chat. The tide was ebbing slowly now and the anchor rope had straightened out, so two of the rods were reeled in and fitted with 2-ounce leads in order to fish more or less straight down under the boat. The other two rods, with lighter weights, were several yards astern. We each drank a cup of coffee and talked of fishing.

A slow dragging pull took a few inches of line from my goby-baited rod. I picked it up and for a moment it felt as though it was snagged. Then it slowly came free but the rod was bent with a weight much greater than that of the 1-ounce lead. 'Crab,' I muttered and began the slow wind to the surface. Harry picked up the landing net and the torch. As he shone the torch in the direction indicated by the line and into the water, six feet down a brownish blur was visible. Gradually it took the form of a large, red-eyed, purple-clawed velvet swimming crab. Harry lifted it into the boat and shook it out of the net. Its rear paddles clattered on the bottom of the boat and it scuttled under the stern seat where it braced its legs against the boards and held up its claws in the characteristic threat. I picked up the crab and dropped it over the side. My goby was mashed to pulp so I replaced it with a fillet of pouting and cast again.

We had been so absorbed in dealing with the crab that neither of us had noticed Harry's multiplier clicking gently. Now, in the silence, it sounded like the ticking of a grandmother clock. As

Harry reached out and picked it up the clicking accelerated, and two feet of line ran quickly from the spool. The sound of the ratchet ceased and I said, 'Has it dropped the bait?' 'I don't think so,' replied Harry and, as he spoke, the fish began to run again, steadily this time. A turn of the handle set the multiplier in gear and as the rod curved smoothly to the pull of the running fish, he struck hard. It was well hooked and began to dive away, swimming with the flow and steadily taking line against the firmly set check. As the run slowed down Harry raised the rod and retrieved a little line by pumping. Each lift of the rod now regained a few feet of line and the fish, still resisting heavily, planed from side to side.

I switched on the big rubber torch and took the piece of protective rubber tubing off the point of the gaff. In the light of the torch the clear shape of a fish was already visible a couple of yards behind the dinghy. 'It's a ray,' we shouted simultaneously. Instantly the fish took on a new importance; it was our first ray. Harry steered the fish carefully round his other line and drew it towards the boat. I plunged the gaff through its wing in the angle between the tail and the body and lifted it into the boat.

Had the boat been larger we would have jumped for joy! The hook was in the corner of the ray's mouth and was easily removed. On Harry's spring balance the fish registered $10\frac{1}{2}$-pounds, a female thornback and quite distinct from the small-eyed ray which we had previously seen.

On subsequent trips we came to realise that thornbacks were one of the less common species on the sandy bed of Swanage Bay. We were now aware of one mark on which rays could be caught and also that at least two species were present in the area. In fact, as we later found, the fish could just as easily have been any one of half-a-dozen species: spotted rays, blonde rays, small-eyed rays, thornbacks, undulate rays and even small (very small) common skate were present in the area at times.

This considerable variety of similar species fascinated us, and for several years ray fishing became one of our main interests. In general, rays are regarded, correctly, as scent feeders, finding their prey primarily by way of the chemicals which it exudes into the water. All of them however have good-sized eyes and many species have a well developed electrical sense. The thornback, for example, has been shown to be capable of detecting the electrical activity due to the breathing muscles of a resting plaice.

Quite a bit of information is available regarding the feeding and the preferred foods of the different species. The food of rays changes dramatically with size and for convenience we have drawn a distinction between small fish of less than 18-inches in length and more desirable larger specimens.

The small spotted ray shows only a slight shift in emphasis of its diet. Ragworms and hoppers (amphipods) are important food items in fish of all sizes, but with rather more crab and sand eel in the larger specimens. The thornback shows a much greater change, with smaller fish feeding mainly on shrimps and porcelain crabs, while the larger ones eat a high proportion of swimming

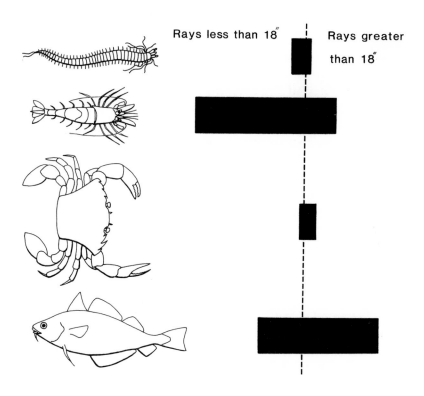

Rays less than 18″   Rays greater than 18″

40. Food of the small-eyed ray. Large fish eat a much greater proportion of crabs and other fishes.

crabs and various types of fish. The blonde ray is chiefly a fish eater and 63 per cent of all the fish up to 4-feet in length contained mostly sand eels. The general pattern is one of a change from ragworms, shrimps and hoppers in small rays to increasing proportions of fish and larger crabs in the older, larger fish.

The original ledge mark on which we had taken the first thornback came to be referred to in later years as the 'skate mark' because it was a prolific source of several species of ray. In the year following our first modest success we were able to fish regularly on two or three evenings each week because Stan (one of our mates) allowed us to use his 11-foot fibreglass and marine-ply dinghy.

In the following May, one evening after tea, Harry and I were once again to be seen piling Barbour jackets, rods, gaffs, tackle bags, oars (3), ropes, cushions (essential) and concrete-filled one-gallon plastic containers which we used as anchors, out of the car and onto the slipway. Harry went to park the car and then the two of us, one lifting the bow and the other the stern of the boat, staggered down the ramp to the water's edge. As we stumbled down the slipway, we muttered phrases such as, 'Either this damn boat's getting heavier or I am getting weaker.' Then, 'Isn't it time we got a launching trolley?' The rowlocks were fitted and tied in place, the anchor rope tied on and coiled in the bow, the tackle was carefully stowed and we set out on the one-mile row to the mark. Harry had already set up his spinning rod armed with a 1-ounce lead and a small Mepps three feet behind it; this he trolled on the way out, taking a mackerel and two small pollack before we anchored up.

Allowing for the wind and tide we shipped the oars and lowered the anchor 'stones' to the sea bed. One stone was sufficient for a neap tide but on this particular night two were tied on about six feet apart to cope with the run of the spring tide and the stiff breeze. Once the anchor rope had drawn tight we checked the position of the marks. Because of the wind we had miscalculated slightly so we hauled up the anchors and moved until we were spot on. This may seem ridiculous, but to eliminate the effect of position from the complicated considerations of time, tide, weather and bait, it was essential.

Even though we had already caught a mackerel the first job

was to fish for some more bait. We had already established to our own satisfaction that neither frozen squid, frozen fish nor fresh mackerel held any advantage over freshly-caught pouting, poor cod or gobies when it came to catching rays or conger. With hindsight, our eventual average of about one good fish per trip, almost all taken on pouting, seems to bear this out.

Bait catching involved the use of light paternosters or legers baited with worm, squid or mackerel strip. During the hours of daylight small wrasse took the worms but as soon as the sun fell below the horizon the pouting began to feed. During the wait for small fish to bite, two additional rods were baited, one with a small squid and the other with a fillet of mackerel; both were lowered to the sea bed and the rods secured, well inboard, with the checks set lightly. In catching bait-fish we had found that a smear of pilchard oil on the worms helped to attract pouting, as did a certain amount of bait movement.

The tidal current was running very hard and, even with 2-ounces of lead, the lines angled away from the stern. Lines of about 18-pounds B.S. were being used for the larger fish because, although rocks were fairly close at hand, even conger rarely went to ground. Provided wire traces were used few fish had been lost on snags, nor indeed by any form of breakage. In the fast-flowing water, every few minutes one or other of the baits would be attacked by crabs, some of which were of good size. Frequently this resulted in a badly torn bait and several times a crab was lifted a few feet from the sea bed before it let go. Already Harry had boated two which had been retained for eating. A large spider crab had also been brought to the net; the span of its legs was almost 18-inches and it had tucked them up into the form of a tight basket as it was picked up and returned. After an hour or so of crab activity bait was beginning to run low and there was some relief when a sharp bite on Harry's heavier rod resulted in a pouting of about 1½-pounds, plenty to keep us going for the evening.

The ratchet of my light rod began to click as the spool slowly rotated, the tide was easing off and the boat, swinging on its anchor rope, was drawing line off the reel. On picking up the rod I found the tackle solidly wedged. Taking the line in my gloved hand I pulled steadily and the tension eased smoothly as it came free, a quite different feeling from the 'ping' of a parting knot. On retrieving the tackle I found the bait gone and the point of the hook slightly turned. I resharpened it, baited up with a large pouting fillet and again lowered the tackle to the sea bed.

As I looked up, Harry was holding the lighter of his rods at the ready. 'What is it?' I asked. 'Not a skate or a conger,' said Harry. 'Just one fast pull. There it is again!' and, as he spoke, he lifted the rod tip sharply in an answering strike. The fish bored away; again and again it dived steeply, pulling the little rod into a deep curve and twice even plunging the tip beneath the waves. Clearly it was not a very big fish, for between the dives Harry was easily regaining line. As the fish neared the boat we saw the rounded silver outline of a black bream. Once in the net we noted that the fish was a female, in characteristic brownish and silver livery, its belly swollen with eggs. The mouth of the bream seemed scarcely large enough to have absorbed the whole squid and 4/0 hook but it was hooked well down. Had we known it at the time, the catching of this fine 2-pound fish on a whole squid was to prove significant in later years of dinghy fishing.

For half-an-hour things went quiet, with not even a crab or pouting bite to relieve the stillness. Even the reliable old cup of undrinkable coffee had failed to produce any action. While we drank our coffee we talked and laughed about Trevor's experience the previous weekend. Having lost a snagged folding anchor on an earlier trip he decided to attach a second, buoyed, line to his expensive new anchor so that, should the event recur, he would be able to 'pull up the hook' from a different direction. He and his wife were contentedly anchored up in his 10-foot Romany plastic dinghy, bottom fishing for rays, about two hundred yards out from Swanage Pier. The action had been very quiet and there were no signs of any fish. 'Perhaps they will come on later when the tide turns,' said Trevor. As he spoke, the line on his Alvey reel started running off. The clicks from the ratchet sounded like a machine gun. 'It must be a tope,' he shouted. 'I've got a bite as well,' said his wife. 'Perhaps it's the same fish.' As Trevor picked up his rod, he suddenly realised that the line was running from his reel because the boat was moving. Not only was it moving but it was travelling at a steady four or five knots, far faster than it had ever gone before. He looked over the prow of the boat to see his

A 10-pound small-eyed ray taken on legered pouting over a sandy sea bed in 30 feet of water.

anchor rope stretched tautly in the direction of a large motor boat, taking a full load of holidaymakers on a tour of Swanage Bay. He shouted to the boatman who was looking the other way and obviously could not hear.

He frantically waved his hands in the direction of the motor boat and all the holidaymakers in the pleasure craft cheerfully waved back. One could almost hear them saying, 'What a nice friendly fellow in that little boat that's following us.' After a good four or five minutes the boatman realised what had happened, slowed down and released the buoyed line attached to the anchor. Immediately Trevor and his wife set off for the shore, vowing to substitute a tripped anchor on the next outing.

Still no action—Harry and I had reeled in and changed to fresh baits; there were pouting fillets on all four rods now. It is good practise to change baits at intervals of twenty to thirty minutes in any event, so as to maintain a strong scent trail. Five minutes after the baits had settled, the reels on both of the heavier rods began to give line simultaneously. 'Could be the boat swinging again,' murmured Harry, but as one man we picked up our rods and gently fingered the lines in an attempt to determine what was going on below.

I told Harry that I could feel the taut nylon twitch at intervals of two to three seconds. 'This is a fish as well,' came his reply and, as if in confirmation, the line began to run steadily off the spool of his lightly-thumbed multiplier. My fish had also moved off and the coils of line were slipping over the edge of the spool and out between my index finger and thumb. I lowered the rod slightly to give an extra foot or two of line as I brought over the bale arm of the reel. The line tightened again and the rod began to bend as the weight of the fish made itself felt. I struck firmly and felt the solid resistance of a decent fish. Looking up, I could see that Harry was also into something sizeable.

My fish began to swim uptide towards the bow of the boat where the slanting anchor rope was visible. I leaned heavily on the rod and managed to turn the fish, only to find that Harry's line had swung across the stern and was now close to mine. My fish was clearly less of a handful than Harry's and I was now making good progress. 'Wait until I get mine into the boat and I'll give you a hand,' I said. The fish was already on the surface, a small-eyed ray of about 8-pounds with the trace looped around the base of its tail. I lifted it by the tail and swung it into the boat. Laying down the rod I picked up the gaff and the torch; a long white shape gleamed faintly far below and Harry's rod bowed and the line sang as the fish plunged away again. 'It looks like a nice conger,' I said. 'Take it easy.' But no such advice was needed and the fish was slowly but surely brought up to the surface where it spun gracefully in the current five yards astern.

Swinging the rod round to starboard, Harry recovered line until the conger was alongside. The gaff was in and I lifted the squirming eel inboard. Harry put down the rod, picked up a blue nitro-chalk sack into which I dropped the fish off the gaff, cut the line above the trace and tied the mouth of the sack with a piece of orange corlene twine brought along for that purpose. Before Harry could tackle up again his other rod, which was still fishing, began to nod as another fish ran swiftly off with the bait. This time we were better organised and after a battle of about five minutes a second small-eyed ray of 11½-pounds was in the fish box.

As we rowed back across the bay, guided by the red light on the pier end, the green phosphorescence shone in the wake and on the tips of the oars. We were well satisfied.

Already we were familiar with the black bream by virtue of the occasional small specimen taken while we were trying to catch bait or as recounted above, on a large bait (usually squid), intended for rays or conger. These sporadic catches were sufficient to suggest that the reputation of these little fish as stout battlers was well deserved. No systematic attempts had been made to catch bream but we had already managed to learn a little about the fish and its habits.

The guts of the bream which we had caught were always full of marine algae, usually stuff which resembled strips of sea lettuce, looking almost as though it had been cut up for a salad. Most of the fish which we caught were females, many of them obviously on the verge of spawning or recently spent. Only once or twice in fact had we caught a male fish, fine dark-banded creatures with a bluish cast to their heads and yellow spectacle markings across their foreheads.

Each year the shoals of bream arrive on their rather localised inshore spawning areas. The male fish are larger than the females, this size difference between the sexes suggesting that, like the ballan wrasse, these fish may undergo a sex change. Many breams are potentially hermophrodites. The male black bream lays claim to an area of the sea bed which it sweeps clear of sand and gravel. This will be the 'nest' on which the female will lay its eggs. The males guard their chosen nesting areas jealously, driving away fish, lobsters, crabs and other intruders.

Our first *catch* of bream came, as is so often the case, more or less by accident. Terry and I had decided to have an early season trip in search of a specimen small-eyed ray. The place which we chose to fish was further offshore than the usual ledge mark. For a couple of seasons previously we had gradually extended our field of operations seawards along the supposed line of the ledge which we had at first detected.

The 'heavy' rods were set up, baited with whole small squid and we set about the usual business of catching bait. An hour passed and nothing was forthcoming with the exception of a couple of swimming crabs. As the sun began to go down in a red haze the boat swung on its anchor line and the tide began to ebb. Terry's ragworm, streaming in the current five fathoms below, was at once taken with a couple of purposeful tugs. The subsequent fight left no doubt as to what he had hooked. Seven or eight times his Milbro Ghillie Salmon spinning rod bent double as the fish struggled to return to the sea bed. After a few minutes, however, the strength and elasticity of the 8-pound B.S. line proved too much and a superb hen black bream of over 2-pounds was netted and lifted inboard.

In the following half hour, seven more bream of between $1\frac{3}{4}$- and $2\frac{1}{2}$-pounds were boated, all having taken ragworm. Before darkness fell, we took careful note of shore marks so that it would be possible to find the exact spot again. As we later established by the use of a portable echo sounder, the mark on which the bream were taken was a depression of the sea bed eighteen inches to two feet below the surrounding area and only twenty to thirty yards across. Rarely did the 'bream mark' let us down and every year early April would find us rowing out to the same spot on the top of a spring tide, confident that on the ebb we would catch bream.

The bream caught in April are invariably of good size but, as the season progresses, the average weight becomes smaller. Seemingly (just as in the case of salmon returning to the river) the spring fish are the big ones; so, in the black bream, it is the large fish which are the earliest spawners and the precursors of the shoals. In most seasons the first bream bite would come, not on the legered ragworm or squid strip, but on the wire trace and whole squid intended for larger fish. This happened so often that I even took to adding a small, squid-baited hook to trail just behind the big bait. As usual, the compromise failed and the few bream caught in this way did not merit the nuisance of constantly reeling in the 'conger tackle' to check the small hook after every little knock. Nor was it worth the risk of losing a good fish lightly hooked on the bream hook.

Black bream often give the impression of being preoccupied with a certain bait. Thus on one evening Harry, Jon and I fished

Black bream taken on 6-pound lines, light spinning rods, flowing traces and squid strip. The two larger (male) fish weighed 2½-pounds each, about average for late April.

(intentionally) each with a different bait—lugworm, ragworm and squid strip. Using ragworm, I was the only one catching bream. We changed baits, and now Harry, using ragworm, began to catch. By the end of two hours hectic fishing, of the thirty-eight bream caught (all over 1½-pounds) thirty-six had been taken on the ragworm. On other occasions squid strip would be taken to the almost total exclusion of all else. In general, it was found to be good policy to take along both rag and squid whenever possible. Why the black bream should take these baits at all when their normal diet on this mark seemed to be algae, we were never able to decide.

Our approach to bream fishing was generally the same as that recommended by the 'experts'. Fine line, a long trace, size 4 or 6 long-shanked hook and a lead small enough to allow the tackle to bounce steadily down tide. At times groundbaiting seemed to improve catches but, not surprisingly in view of the territorial habits of the fish, it was no substitute for being on exactly the right spot. Most of our fish were caught on the ebb tide, but on the flood we found that it was necessary to anchor sixty yards south of the normal mark if fish were to be caught (i.e. on the other side of the 'bream ground'.) Our groundbait was usually in the form of some sort of breadcrumb mix with pilchard oil, codliver oil, crushed crab, minced fish or in fact almost anything we could lay hands on. A fairly heavy 'duff' was squeezed onto one of the pebbles taken out for the purpose and lumps of the material thus weighted were dropped over the side of the boat at intervals. On one trip, when we had acquired a particularly large bottle of reject codliver oil, the resulting oil slick attracted a group of fulmars which entertained us between bites by dabbling on the surface for drifting bread crumbs.

The usual problem in bream fishing off Swanage is the

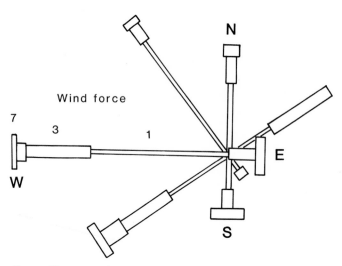

41.   Wind forces and direction at Swanage over a year. East and south-east winds are infrequent but strong and often interfere with dinghy fishing for black bream in April and May.

weather. The prevailing wind off this coast is from the south and west and from these quarters the bay is very sheltered. May, however, is a period when east winds can be expected and the slightest breath of east (onshore) wind means no fishing from small boats. At times it seemed almost as though landing the first bream of the year was a signal for an easterly blow. If the wind changed to the east when we were already at sea, conditions could quickly become very dangerous, even for craft larger than ours, and any hint of an onshore blow was indicative of the need for an 'early bath', whatever the fish were doing.

Not all the hazards of dinghy fishing were due to mother nature. It was on a fine calm night that Harry and I set out after bream, as usual full of anticipation. As I pulled away from the slipway everything seemed right but about a hundred yards out I said, 'There seems to be a lot of water in the bottom of the boat tonight.' A closer inspection showed that there was a neat hole of about two inches diameter just below the water line. A fountain of water was spurting elegantly into the air and rapidly equalising the levels inside and out. We looked at each other in dismay and, as one man, leaned over to port thus raising the offending hole above the water surface. Harry produced a large plastic bag which we stuffed into the hole and wedged in place with the butt end of a gaff. With the flow thus abated we baled out the excess moisture and made a joint declaration not to let it spoil the night. We then proceeded, on a rather uneven keel, to the 'bream mark' and eventually managed to land a 20-pound conger, using the ever-present spare gaff.

After that day the hull was examined with scrupulous care before every trip. We were later informed that the 'little perforation' had been caused by a carelessly parked motor bike which had fallen onto our cockleshell: the offender had not thought it worthwhile to leave a note to inform us.

12

'O Sole mio!'

SOLE AND OTHER FLAT FISH

As a group, the flat fishes show a variety of feeding habits almost as great as that of all other species put together. They range from the burrowing bottom-grubbing soles to full-blown, fish-eating predators like the halibut and the turbot. They have in common a very compressed body and a coloured eyed-side which together provide them with a camouflage superior even to that of the renowned chameleon.

From the angler's point of view, the flat fishes alone could provide more than a lifetime of interest. Certainly in the Poole area, flounder, plaice, dab and common sole are all much sought after both for sport and for eating.

With regard to angling for that popular species, the flounder, it would be difficult to better the book *Sea Angling with the Baited Spoon*, written by John Garrad. Any angler, whatever his quarry and whether he fishes in the sea or fresh waters, could do worse than follow Garrad's example of how to evaluate and develop a single method of fishing. As far as we are aware, no one has continued Garrad's experiments with the baited spoon, despite the fact that his reported catches of flounders were probably better, and certainly more consistent than any reported before or since. This apathy is all the more surprising in view of the fact that Garrad was at pains to suggest how other species might respond to the enormous variety of lures which he tested.

In no way could we claim to be as knowledgeable about flat fish as Garrad, nor indeed as many other anglers. Nonetheless some of our experiences may be of interest to others. At one time or another we have fished for and caught most of the common species. Before giving any details it is probably worthwhile to provide a fairly detailed account of scientific studies on the feeding of flat fish in the light of which some of our observations and those of others may be seen in perspective. The sea angler may find interesting some experiments carried out on the feeding behaviour of several common species. The idea of this work was to see which factors were responsible for stimulating feeding. In these experiments the 'prey' presented to the fish was in the form of models and scents and/or tastes (hereafter referred to as taste).

The models used were spheres of 1, 2, 4 and 8 centimetres diameter, a small model fish and a plastic shrimp. The spheres were simply meant to represent 'food' items of different sizes and from our point of view they could scarcely be better because lead weights of equivalent volume would weigh about $\frac{1}{4}$ oz. $1\frac{1}{2}$ oz, $\frac{3}{4}$ lb. and $6\frac{1}{2}$ lb. The largest would perhaps be a little on the large side even for a fast tide on the Skerries Banks, but even so the sizes are of the right order. The scents used were the juices of mussel or shrimp and (for experiments with turbot and brill) the juices of sole or cucumber smelt.

The first tests were made with the sole—a highly specialised, nocturnal-feeding, flat fish with a very well developed sense of touch on the underside of the head.

The sole was *attracted* to the three smaller spheres and to the plastic shrimp but it *panicked* at the sight of the largest sphere. In all cases the attractiveness of the models was increased by the presence of mussel or shrimp juice in the water. Significantly the sole also showed a strong panic reaction to the presence of a small codling in its tank.

The sole, although it is almost exclusively a night feeder, uses its powers of both vision and taste to locate its prey. As in the case of the fifteen-spined stickleback mentioned earlier, the effects of each stimulus were increased by the presence of another.

It is perhaps surprising that the plaice, the flounder and the dab (unlike the sole) showed no interest in any of the spheres, expressing neither feeding nor flight reactions. Occasionally all three species would approach and snap at the plastic shrimp but *only* when it was moving. In fact, the dab even swallowed the shrimp in one instance. In contrast, when the juices of mussel or shrimp were in the water all three swam up to, and even bit at the spheres.

A second set of tests, also with plaice, flounder and dab, were

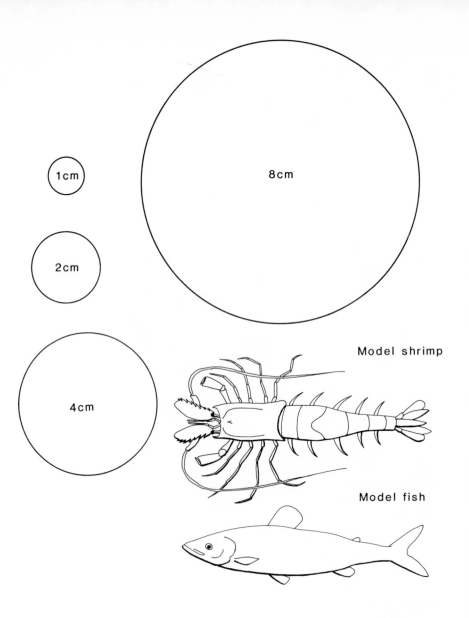

1cm

2cm

4cm

8cm

Model shrimp

Model fish

42.   Spheres, model shrimps and model fish used to test the feeding behaviour of various flat fishes. All were used with or without the added juices of mussel, shrimp, sole or smelt.

designed to see how good these fish were at locating their food. To do this a fine jet of sea water was squirted from a tiny glass tube, the tip of which projected just above the surface of the sand on the bottom of the tank. The plaice was the only one of the three to react to a plain jet of water. Plaice, it should be noted, often feed on the siphon tubes of burrowing clams, tubes from which little jets of water are constantly being pumped by the molluscs. When *very dilute* shrimp-juice was added to the water-jet, both the plaice and the flounder located and bit at the end of the glass tube. The dab was unable to locate the tube and just swam about aimlessly snapping its jaws. It clearly sensed the shrimp-juice and when the 2-cm sphere was presented it promptly attacked it. The dab is by nature a more active hunter than either flounder or plaice, eating shrimps and similar fast-swimming creatures. All three fish are essentially daytime hunters in which both sight and taste are important.

G.A. Steven, in his interesting account of the feeding of the 'lemon sole', which is scarcely an angler's fish, describes how this fish is a specialist worm-feeder and pounces from a 'head in air' position vertically down on the worms as they emerge cautiously from their sea-bed burrows. In this account he mentions that the plaice is not nearly so good at catching worms because it attacks by swimming with its body horizontal and its head close to the sea bed. The dab, which is much more active than either, takes up an intermediate posture with its head slightly raised in an alert fashion. It feeds on a much wider range of food items.

Returning to the feeding experiments, the turbot and the brill are closely related and very similar. They are active daytime feeders, mainly eating fish. Both species ignored the three smaller spheres even when mussel, shrimp or fish juice were in the water, nor did they show any reaction to the juices alone. As in the case of the sole, the largest sphere caused a very strong flight (panic) reaction. Fish which were previously buried in the sand came out and swam quickly away. The conclusion would seem to be: when fishing for turbot or brill, beware the use of short traces, which place the bait too close to large leads.

If they were moving, models of fish were approached and snapped at by turbot and brill. Moving plastic shrimps were also attacked, but neither mussel, shrimp nor fish juice enhanced the feeding behaviour.

Generally, sight feeders such as turbot, bass, pollack or mackerel, react only to something that *looks and moves right* (i.e. like the normal prey) and not to mere lumps of material such as rough old chunks of bait. They may even be terrified of large non-food objects such as lead weights.

The structures of the brains and in particular of the guts of the flat fishes considered above bear out the observations described. The fish feeders have larger mouths and stomachs and shorter intestines than the other species. The gill rakers (comb-like teeth on the inner edges of the gills) of the turbot and the brill are few and large and serve to prevent the escape of large prey through the gill openings. In contrast, fish such as the sole, which feed on bottom-living animals containing a large proportion of indigestible material, have small mouths and stomachs, very long intestines and small, fine gill rakers. Dab, plaice and flounder fall into an intermediate group.

To put into perspective some of the behaviour described, it is worthwhile having a look at the food of the species considered. When possible the results are separated into small and large fish as was done for rays.

The common sole is unquestionably a nocturnal feeder which,

43. Turbot, flounder and sole. Relative proportions of the gut used for (1) capturing and holding food (mouth and stomach) and (2) digesting food (intestines).

during the daylight hours, remains buried in the sand, moving little. Observations made by W. Bateson in 1890 are also of great interest to the angler in search of these strange little fish. He describes how the sole creeps about the sea bed using its fringe of fin rays almost like the legs of a millipede. As it moves slowly along it gently pats the sand with its head, with the sense organs on its blind side feeling for objects lying on the surface. The sole only succeeds in finding food which lies on the sea bed and will not notice material suspended above it. Even the mouth of the sole is positioned so as to facilitate picking up objects from the bed of the sea.

Associated with its cryptic behaviour and specialised way of feeding, quite a lot of work has been done on the chemical senses of the sole. Young soles weaned from live brine shrimps would only eat an artificial diet when it was flavoured with the juice of the mussel or with the substance Glycine-betaine, a component of mussel juice. Both detection and selection of food items depend on this chemical. Various amino acids are also involved in recognition of food, both in small sole and in other fish. Glycine-betaine is a true feeding stimulant for sole, because its presence increases food consumption over a long period of time. The worms, small molluscs and crustaceans on which the sole feeds are known to contain large amounts of this feeding stimulant and the fish has a special sense for detecting it. The Glycine-betaine is absent from the flesh of fish (other than dogfish and rays) so attractants such as pilchard oil are, presumably, useless for sole.

The sole is quite a slow-growing fish and takes ten to fifteen years to reach about 15-inches in length. The fish are in poor condition in June and July but reach a peak in the autumn and winter.

In our limited experience of fishing for sole, an interesting series of observations led us to an approach subtly different to the one which we used at first. It was clear that sole were to be caught in the autumn and at night from the sandy, rather featureless, beaches off Bournemouth and Swanage. Harry and I, keen to catch one of these gourmet's delights, fished with long traces, small hooks and worm baits, much as we had been accustomed to do for flounder and plaice. The results were, to say the least, pathetic. We caught a few flounders, some small plaice,

tiny school bass, poor cod and more poor cod. We would cast out
and retrieve slowly across the sand as was our custom and, every
minute or two we would catch a poor cod, or sometimes, a
pouting.

The answer was revealed to us by Fred Philpott who, during a
stay at Lowestoft, had specialised in catching plaice and sole. Fred
was full of confidence when we told him of our desire to catch a
sole. 'No problem,' he said. Disbelieving, we said we would wait
until the fish was under the grill before we were convinced. On
the following Monday as we arrived at work, there was Fred
with a fine 2-pound plaice and (wonder of wonders) a $\frac{3}{4}$-pound
sole. We were incredulous. 'Where did you get them?' The reply
was even more surprising: Fred had spent the Sunday afternoon
and evening fishing from the same stretch of beach on which

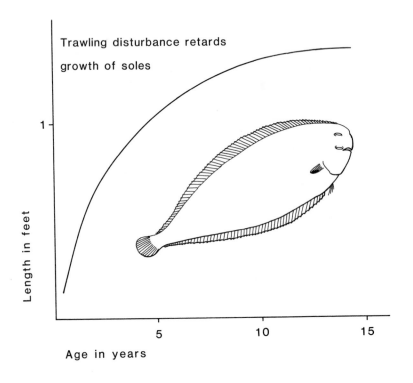

Trawling disturbance retards

growth of soles

Length in feet

Age in years

44.   Growth of the common sole (aged by otoliths).

Harry and I had waged our campaign on the uncatchable sole. We were astounded but, the following Wednesday, our astonishment grew to the proportions of hero worship when the indomitable Fred produced two more sole of 1-pound and 2½-pounds. 'How do you do it?' we asked. 'Legered lugworm,' came the reply. 'What do you mean, legered lugworm?' we said. 'We've fished lug and rag for hours and all we catch are pouting and poor cod!'

The next time Fred went fishing for flatfish, Harry and I were with him. We inspected Fred's tackle minutely as he set it up. It was virtually identical to our own. A simple paternoster with a flowing trace and a long-shanked No. 1 hook baited with a plump lugworm. The hook was a fraction larger than ours but this seemed unlikely to make any difference. We arranged ourselves along the beach and cast out our respective tackles. Harry and I stood holding the rods, retrieving slowly and feeling carefully for the slightest hint of interest from a sole. Fred cast out, propped the rod on its rest and lay down on the beach.

Every couple of minutes Harry or I would, as normal, get a rattling bite, strike, and reel in a poor cod, a small bass, even an 8-ounce flounder. For over an hour Fred lay, practically immobile, the back of his head cradled in his interlocked fingers. Occasionally he would whistle a tune or crack a joke but, in the main, he was motionless. As Harry was reeling in his twentieth or so, 2-ounce poor cod, Fred stood up. 'There's a knock,' he said and a little later he picked up his beach caster. A minute or more after this he struck hard and reeled in a ½-pound common sole, the only one caught that night. The answer to the conundrum was staring us in the face—*presentation*. Harry and I, constantly alert and searching the sea bed with fingers on the trigger, were really geared up to attracting the actively-hunting school bass and pouting. Fred's inert lugworm on the other hand was tailor-made to avoid these nuisance fish and tempt the sniffing, pitpatting soles.

On later trips we adapted our methods and even managed to catch some sole from the beaches we had fished unsuccessfully for years. By leaving the worms to fish quietly for themselves, the number of pout bites was reduced enormously and our intended quarry had time to find and take the baits. Even the movement of

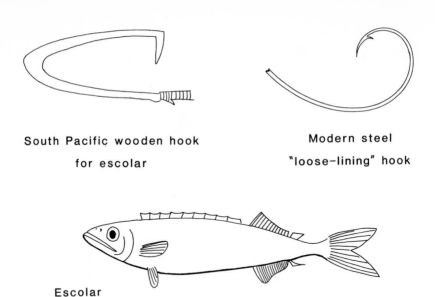

South Pacific wooden hook
for escolar

Modern steel
"loose-lining" hook

Escolar

45.   Special wooden hook, effective on loosely set long lines used for escolar. A similar design could be effective for sole.

a lively ragworm seemed sufficient to attract pouting and, perhaps for this reason, lug was a better bait for sole. We will, I fear, never be good sole fishermen, the essential enthusiasm is lacking, but these fascinating fish gave us an object lesson in the importance of bait presentation.

To those who wish to try 'lazing' for sole, there is a technique devised by the natives of the South Pacific for fish called escolar which might be of interest. The fish are caught on set ground lines which lie loosely on the sea bed. The key to success is a specially fashioned wood hook with an inturned point. Scientific tests involving modern long lines for deep sea fish compared the value of metal hooks of normal design and others based on the design of the escolar hook. The latter were *much* more successful and it would seem that a similar pattern could be worth a try for the sedentary sole.

Now we can take a look at the flounder, which can be found in fresh and salt water and feeds actively in both. Although the amount of time which we have spent fishing for flounder is small, we have caught comparatively large numbers of these fish. Locations vary from the waters of a large chalk stream—the River Frome (five miles upstream of the tidal limits) to the estuary downstream of Wareham and out over the broad grey mudflats of Poole Harbour. Also we have fished along the dune-backed sandy beaches of Studland and the holiday beaches of Bournemouth, Swanage and Weymouth.

Generally the flounder is a very obliging fish and during the spawning migration of the adults from rivers to the sea, which takes place in autumn and early winter, large numbers are caught in estuaries. For example, many flounders are caught at this time by anglers fishing from the quays and river banks in the upper tidal limits of the Frome at Wareham. Many of the fish caught are undersized and obviously immature, which suggests that there might be a sort of dummy spawning run by these young fish. Legered earthworm or, even better, ragworm are successful baits in this situation and the former is effective well up into fresh water, with fish of up to $1\frac{1}{2}$-pounds in weight being taken at times. Legered or paternostered ragworm is also effective in the sea and harbour and anglers casting from the muddy and sandy shores make large bags of good fish, particularly in winter. The trolled baited-spoon method is effective in summer and, some years ago, I took a number of flounders using this technique. Flounders eat numbers of other fish and, using unbaited spinners, we have taken quite a few both from the river and the sea. One such catch which included seven fish over a pound, all taken in an hour-and-a-half, was made using a No. 3 Mepps Mino. Some good flounders have also been caught on live minnows fished for trout and sea trout.

Fishing from the pier at Swanage, Harry and I have taken numerous good-sized flounders in both winter and spring, using ragworm as the bait and traditional techniques. The fish caught ranged up to $2\frac{1}{4}$-pounds. On a few occasions we used peeler crab (when it was available) for bait and it resulted in a dramatic improvement in catches both in numbers and in size. Substitution of crab for worm sometimes salvaged long biteless periods by

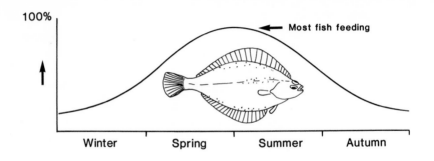

100% ← Most fish feeding

Winter   Spring   Summer   Autumn

46.   Seasonal variation in the proportion of flounders having full stomachs. The fish feed most actively in the warmer months of the year.

producing one or two fish in quick succession.

Flounders will feed in almost unbelievably shallow water (as little as 2-3 inches deep) and even large fish can be caught when the tide begins to flood over sandy beaches and mud banks. The angler must be prepared to put up with a certain amount of scorn and derision from bystanders if he is to make the best of the tide. He must cast a few yards only, into shallow drainage gulleys, as the water begins to creep from the deep channels into which the fish retreat at low water. In the early 1960s I spent three years studying the animals of the sand and mudflats on the coast of Northumberland. During that time I caught numerous flounders using a 7-foot spinning rod and 6-pound line. Retreating before the rapidly advancing tide and casting into the water at my feet I took fish of all sizes on worm, cockle, mussel and crab, but the largest fish, a 3½-pounder, was landed on a freelined live sand eel.

A species which seems to have a similar behaviour pattern to our flounder is the American 'winter flounder'. Observations made on this fish by using underwater television showed that the winter flounder surges into the intertidal zone in a short period two to two-and-a-half hours after low tide. Later, on the tide, the fish spread out and are presumably less easy to find and catch. Between the tide marks is the major feeding area of the winter flounder.

Flounders spawn in the sea in early spring and peak numbers of flounder larvae occur in March and April. In summer large numbers of tiny 'postage stamps' can be seen swimming over the stony bed of the River Frome estuary or inching their way along the vertical walls of quaysides and bridges as though they had been licked and stuck down.

The flounder is in peak condition (fattest) in the period from June to July; conversely, they are thin and in poor condition from February to April, after spawning. In relation to this the fish feed more actively in summer than in winter and almost twice as many of the fish netted from the Tamar estuary in the summer months had full stomachs compared to those taken in winter. The main foods of the flounder are shore crabs, worms and small fish.

The plaice is a close relative of the flounder but is much more a species of the open sea. Both can be caught by using similar bottom-fishing methods. The plaice is a fairly specialised feeder on small 'clams' of various sorts. The smallest fish (too small to be taken on rod and line) graze, like tiny marine sheep, on the thin projecting siphons of tellins (clams) or the probing, searching tentacles of burrowing worms. Molluscs make up 25 per cent of the diet of the larger fish. Young plaice, at least, feed mostly in the daylight hours between sunrise and sunset.

Plaice are important commercially and the species has received more than its fair share of study, little of which is of any direct importance to anglers. The growth of the plaice varies in different parts of its range and, as might be expected, is better where the food supply is good. There are however, different races of plaice which inherit the tendency to grow slowly or quickly. This has been shown by transplanting fast-growing North Sea fish into the Baltic, where the fish are slow-growing. It is also generally well known that the size of plaice is broadly related to water depth and that large plaice are found in deeper water than smaller fish.

Like the sole, plaice which are travelling long distances have been shown to leave the bottom at slack water and drift or swim downstream with the current until the next slack water when they return to the sea bed.

The plaice spawns in winter and large numbers of the larvae occur in January, February and March. The fish spawn in a few restricted areas, one of the main ones being at the east end of the English Channel. The spawning grounds are always such that the eggs and larvae will be carried by the prevailing currents towards sandy, nursery beaches.

Other than the occasional plaice which we caught by bottom-fishing with worm, fish-strip or squid and large numbers of plaice between a ½- and ¾-pound taken whilst flounder fishing from sandy beaches, we made only one serious attempt to catch plaice in quantity. We fished over a sandy bottom in about two fathoms of water at a spot from which there had been recent reports of good catches. We fished for equal lengths of time with legered and with floatfished ragworm, lugworm, mussel and mackerel strip and both methods took similar numbers of plaice. The only difference in fact was that the float tackle, trotted with the current, took a couple of small brill when a fish-baited hook was suspended a foot from the sea bed.

The dab, as already mentioned, is an active fish feeding chiefly on swimming crustacea. When very young, they feed on mollusc siphons and worm tentacles in the same manner as young plaice. Dabs from the Firth of Forth ate hermit crabs, swimming crabs and hoppers (amphipods) but brittle stars were more important as

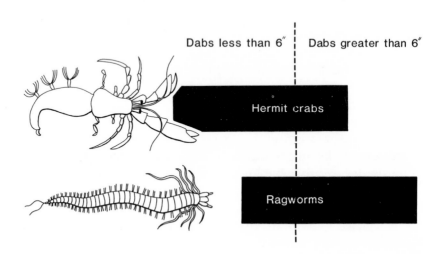

47.   The food of the dab. Large dabs may eat a high proportion of ragworm.

food in St Andrew's Bay. In contrast, another study showed that larger dabs ate more worms.

Dabs are in poor condition (thin) from April to June (after spawning) but they reach their peak from July to December, stopping feeding in winter during their spawning period. In the Baltic, commercial fishing was shown to cause a drastic reduction in the number of older/larger dabs in the population, a good example of the effect of overfishing.

The turbot and the brill are not uncommon around the shores of Britain. Both are highly specialised in terms of habitat, behaviour and food. The brill prefers to live on bottoms of finer sand than those inhabited by the turbot. Even when very young and living close inshore the little turbots favour coarser, gritty sand, but in later life they live further offshore, often on shallow banks of shell gravel, or coarse sand. Both species feed on sand eels and other fishes with an average length-to-thickness ratio of about seven-and-a-half to one.

For several years we spent considerable periods of time fishing for these fish from charter boats, mostly over the Shambles Bank. For the knowledge gained in the course of these trips we are in the debt of our skipper, the late Bert Randall. Most of what we learned from him is entirely consistent with the available information on the biology of this fine fish.

Our first encounter with turbot was, as usual, by chance. It was the eve of Harry's birthday in September and, on the spur of the moment, he decided to treat himself and take a boat-fishing trip from Weymouth. We had never before made such a trip so he looked in the telephone directory, picked out the name of one of the Weymouth skippers and rang the number. Were there any vacancies for the following day? The skipper said he was taking out a part of regulars but there was room for just one more.

The morning of the fateful birthday dawned bright and clear. Harry took along his own tackle but, because of his inexperience, when he discovered that free tackle was provided he decided to take advantage of the offer. The skipper was Bert Randall and the trip was the first of many. On the way out, Harry, always a good listener, was all ears concerning the fishing out of Weymouth.

On the Shambles the water depth over the shell gravel dunes is only a few fathoms at low water spring tides. Just beyond the banks the water falls sharply away to over twenty fathoms. Harry learned of the complex currents around Portland Bill and of the different species to be caught in the area.

During the outward journey from Weymouth Harbour the mackerel lines, some with heavy leads, some with paravanes, were trolled to provide a supply of fresh bait. On this day the mackerel were, for once, plentiful and soon the *Sea Fisher* was anchored close to the old lightship (now redundant) which used to mark the position of the bank. They came to rest just uptide of the large standing waves formed by the tide race over the bank. The bait was long, tapering, thin slices of mackerel, two such baits being cut from either flank of the fish. Each fillet was hooked once through its narrow end without being touched by hand, a tricky ritual which Bert always observed. To achieve this he used a unique filleting knife, razor sharp and consisting of a ground-down, industrial hacksaw blade.

Harry examined the tackle, a large centre pin reel, a heavy duty solid glass rod and 60-pound B.S. nylon. At the business end was a Clement's boom and a 12-foot trace of the heavy nylon armed with a 4/0 hook. 'Turbot like a bait with plenty of movement,' Bert explained. 'Let the lead down slowly to avoid tangles.' The lead was bounced away on the current until it was felt to cross the top of a ridge. This approach is, of course, easiest from the stern positions in the boat.

When the tide is really running hard on banks such as the Shambles it becomes virtually impossible to fish at anchor. The normal practice is to fish either side of slack water and to shift the position of the boat so as to take advantage of an hour or more lag in the time of the tide on different parts of the bank. It is only possible to fish tide races such as these under good weather conditions because huge waves, as high as a house, will build up and run along the length of the bank quite without warning. For this reason it is essential to fish these banks with a skipper who is familiar with the unique conditions.

To return to the fishing; Harry was, as he would say, gently bumping his 1-pound lead along the sea bed when he felt a tentative bite. At first it gave the impression of a small fish pulling

A 20-pound turbot from the Shambles bank. A 12-foot flowing trace and mackerel strip was the successful method.

at the bait, then there were two or three strong knocks which
caused him to release a foot or two of line. As he struck, the rod
bent to the pull of a heavy fish which, together with the big lead
and the fast tide, made really hard work of the retrieve. After a
few minutes of arm-stretching line recovery the fish planed to the
surface five yards astern. It was drawn alongside, in went Bert's
gaff and Harry had caught his, and our, first ever turbot, a
speckled beauty of 12-pounds.

The birthday treat went from good to better to fantastic as he
landed four more turbot. He was so pleased that he gave away
one of his fish to a fellow-angler who had come down from
Bristol for the day.

Subsequently, after our first couple of turbot trips, we resorted
to our own tackle. Not only were we able to fish considerably

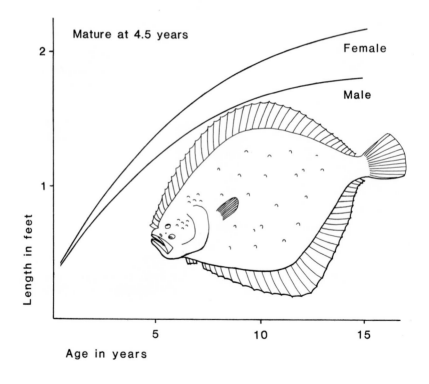

48.   Growth of the turbot (aged by otoliths).

lighter but it was much less effort to spend the day reeling in 2- or 4-ounces of lead instead of $\frac{1}{2}$-pound or a pound. The method used was identical to that already described. A long flowing trace of 30-pound B.S. monofilament, a 4/0 hook and the minimum of lead necessary to maintain contact with the sea bed.

Even when the fishing was slow, a trip with Bert was never dull. He had a seemingly inexhaustible fund of good fishing stories, many of which were an education as well as an entertainment. On one still foggy morning as we motored out towards the banks he recalled a similar trip when he had taken out a party down from the Midlands. The fog had been dense so he asked the anglers to keep a sharp look-out and give a shout if they could see anything. As they approached the Shambles, much to the amusement of all, Bert produced the antique ear trumpet which he used the better to hear the fog sirens of the Shambles Light and Portland Bill. On seeing the ancient instrument the ever-present wag of the party looked across and said in a loud voice to all present, 'I don't know what sort of trip we've let ourselves in for lads, the . . . . . . skipper's deaf as well as blind.'

There followed a series of successful trips during which we landed many turbot up to 20-pounds, plus large brill and blonde rays. One of our workmates, Ian, decided that he would like to have a go. Ian had always been reluctant to put out to sea because he was inclined to suffer from seasickness. Harry, for once, was unable to go but I went along with Ian. The weather conditions were not of the best but, with the odd good turbot and ray coming to the boat it was just enough to take Ian's mind off his internal qualms. When the tide began to run hard the skipper decided on a move; by nipping across the bank it was possible to have an extra hour-and-a-half of fishing in a hundred feet of water on the far side. With the chance of bream, conger and tope on the new mark, I decided on a change of tackle and bait. As I put my hand into my fishing bag and pulled out a couple of small squid, dripping with pilchard oil, the combination of smell and appearance was too much for Ian. His face blanched and then turned a delicate shade of green; he had just sufficient presence of mind to set the check and prop his rod in a safe fishing position before he lost interest in the proceedings.

As Ian hung wretchedly over the stern a denizen of the deeps decided to take an interest in his bait. Being of a helpful disposition I picked up Ian's rod in my left hand, struck hard and offered the rod to my friend who groaned and turned away. All would have been well but, as I was about to lay down my own rod, I felt a sharp knock and line began to pour off the reel. Somehow I managed to check the spinning spool and strike with one hand but now I had a problem; a heavy fish was boring about on the left-hand rod and on the other my adversary was headed for France. The day was saved by a heroic effort from Ian, for he took his own rod and gamely, between bouts of sickness, managed to play and boat a double-header of a $2\frac{1}{2}$-pound black bream and a 12-pound huss. I, meanwhile, struggled with the other fish, a 40-pound tope, which was tailed and returned to the sea.

This is not the first book in which anglers have expressed their gratitude to the late Bert Randall. He will always be remembered by us and many other grateful anglers for his unflagging enthusiasm in pursuit of fish. Perhaps the most memorable of his habits was the way in which he would present a fishless angler with a turbot to take home (caught on Bert's own longline). The fish was often worth far more than the angler had paid for his day's sport. Those were the days!

13

The proof of the pudding

FOUR YEARS' FACTS AND FIGURES

As is usual in books about fishing, we have presented quite a few accounts of angling trips without really trying to indicate whether the fishing described was poor, average or exceptionally good, even though we have included descriptions of the many hours put in for little or no returns. Because of these problems it was felt that a simple record of a few of our angling years might be of interest to others.

How does one judge the quality of fishing? An addict of wreck fishing may consider a 'good trip' to be one on which he catches hundreds of pounds of fish. To achieve such highspots he will, no doubt, spend considerable sums of money on travel, charters and tackle. He is prepared to put in many hours steaming to and from marks for a brief hour or two of hectic sport. The wreck angler also has to contend with cancellations caused by adverse weather, discomfort caused by seasickness and, no doubt at times, even he will meet with less than 100 per cent success.

In complete contrast, the freshwater match fisherman is well satisfied with lesser catches of much smaller, more or less inedible fish. The occasional match-winning catch of perhaps 10-pounds will be a highlight. Again, he may drive many miles for his fishing, buy expensive tackle and buy or breed large quantities of bait and groundbait. He, also, must tolerate the vagaries of the weather in the form of storms and floods.

The pleasures of angling manifest themselves in these and many other guises. Beach matches in our area are often won with a few pounds of fish and there is frequently a high proportion of blanks. In fly fishing for reservoir trout, it is well known that a small proportion of anglers account for most of the catches. The specimen hunter is renowned for the persistence with which he or she will endeavour to catch large fish of a particular species. The salmon fisherman may even spend a season with little to show for it, in anticipation of one day making a bag of several fish or even catching the elusive 40-pounder.

Who would be foolish enough to say that any one of these forms of angling (in most of which we have at times indulged) is 'better' than another? There are as many reasons for enjoying a day's fishing as there are anglers, so the following analysis must be taken for what it is, a simplified description of our efforts to evolve methods which suit us and our area.

So how should one judge results? The weight of fish caught is not much use because the different species vary so much in size. The expenditure of money and time, and the problems of discomfort and inconvenience are common to all forms of angling in some degree. What we want is some sort of measure of success in terms of catch and effort because, however beautiful the scenery, the ultimate satisfaction is that of a good bag of fish.

Because this analysis includes quite a few different anglers the measure of effort used is the *man hour*. For example, a party of ten fishing for one hour on a wreck charter or one man spinning for ten hours from the beach would each represent ten man hours. Success is judged in two ways, firstly the total number of fish caught, which is an indication of the amount of 'action' in an hour, and secondly the numbers of 'good' fish caught. For present purposes 'good' fish are defined in our own terms, because, as we have seen, everyone has his (or her) own criterion according to their aims.

The example used covers four successive years for which we kept detailed records of every trip. Information on time of day, state of tide, weather and so on have already been covered in other chapters. The years dealt with are those during which we divided our time between dinghy fishing, beach casting and spinning/fly fishing from the shore. The results have been looked at in these three categories. A list of the baits used gives some idea of the scope and variety of tactics applied to each.

Dinghy fishing A 10-foot rowing dinghy within about one mile of the shore in Swanage Bay. Usually the methods used were simple one-hook running leger or paternoster.

Beach casting Shores of mud, sand, gravel and rock from Bournemouth to Abbotsbury were fished using methods similar to the above.

The baits used for bottom fishing from dinghy and shore were lugworm, ragworm, mussel, slipper limpet, squid, cuttlefish, soft/peeler crab, sand eel, pouting, mullet, bass, gobies, freshwater eels, lampreys, sand smelts, pollack, herring, mackerel, sprat, kipper, dace, smoked salmon and pork crackling.

Float fishing Quill and balsa floats, both fixed and sliding. The latter were small, streamlined home-made floats, stopped by a small bead and a spade-end stopknot of sewing thread (shifting a nylon stopknot burns and kinks the line.) A small cork makes a handy fixed float if it is slit with a razor blade and pushed onto the line.

Baits fished under a float were lugworm, ragworm, squid, soft/peeler crab, sand eel, pouting, freshwater eel, lamprey, sand smelt, sprat, prawn, shrimp, maggot, bread.

Spinning Spinning from both dinghy and shore covered a wide range of lures which were either trolled, cast and retrieved or jigged as appropriate.

Pirks from $\frac{1}{2}$-ounce to $3\frac{1}{2}$-ounces, Tobys, rubber eels of many types, bar spoons (Mepps and Mepps Mino), bar spoons with balsa wood bodies were constructed and used to fish over shallow weedy ground. Plugs with fixed or adjustable lips, single and two-jointed, ranging from $1\frac{1}{2}$- to 12-inches in length, wooden and plastic Devon minnows. Freshwater eels, dace, strips of many fish species and sand eels.

Fly fishing Fly fishing with trout fly rods from the rocks. Lures used were mackerel feathers, tube flies, streamer flies, wet trout and salmon flies, dry flies, polystyrene flies, rubber squids and blowfly maggots.

Most of these baits are the same as those used by other anglers. A few may seem rather unusual; dace, lampreys and freshwater eels were easily obtainable substitutes for small sea fish such as sand smelts and sand eels. Wooden Devons used for bottom fishing were simply lowered on paternoster tackle and allowed to work in the current. The natural fish were moderately successful baits for bass. The plugs and Devon minnows caught cod, pollack and pouting when used from the dinghy.

The following are what we regard as 'good' fish:

Bass	over 4 lbs
Black Bream	over 2 lbs
Blonde Ray	over 10 lbs
Cod	over 10 lbs
Conger	over 10 lbs
Flounder	over $1\frac{1}{2}$lbs
Mullet (thick-lipped)	over $2\frac{1}{2}$lbs
Plaice	over $1\frac{1}{2}$lbs
Pollack	over 4 lbs
Pouting	over 2 lbs
Sole	over $1\frac{1}{2}$lbs
Small-eyed Ray	over 9 lbs
Thornback Ray	over 10 lbs

Over the four years considered, the number of man-hours fished in each year varied as follows: 740, 482, 520 and 408.

Taking first of all the results of conventional beach fishing a simple table can be used to express the results:

Year	man hours (total)	man hours (per fish)	man hours (per good fish)
1	389	1·5	49
2	182	3·2	45
3	213	1·0	30
4	91	2·7	13
Average	219	2·1	34

TABLE 6   Conventional beach and float fishing.

These beach casting, bait fishing methods, produced a fish roughly every two man-hours. This figure is an underestimate because many of the small fish caught were not recorded in detail.

It is interesting to notice that the time spent in catching a 'good' fish decreased markedly over the four years even though the number of hours fished varied. Thus in the first year we put in 49 hours for each good fish and in the last only 13 hours. The improvement was due to our more critical approach to where and when we fished.

A similar analysis can be presented for spinning/fly fishing methods over the same four year period.

Year	man hours (total)	man hours (per fish)	man hours (per good fish)
1	168	2·5	4·4
2	168	2·6	7·3
3	212	1·6	4·0
4	223	2·8	8·3
Average	193	2·4	6·0

TABLE 7   Spinning and fly fishing from the beach.

The first notable feature of these results is the way in which the number of man-hours increased over the four years from less than half those of conventional methods in year 1 to over twice the number in year 4. There was little variation in the number of man-hours per fish and these averaged out at a slightly higher value than the corresponding beach casting figures. The most striking difference however lies in the number of hours per 'good' fish, which average only six as opposed to thirty-four. The absence of any consistent improvement in the effort needed to catch a 'good' fish is probably due to continually changing methods and the fact that an increasing proportion of time spent in fly fishing and the difficulty of equating a good mullet caught on fly with a good bass caught by spinning.

Before we get carried away with these results it is worth remembering that, normally, all our spinning and fly fishing is done between the months of April and November. If comparisons are restricted to these months it still took three times as long to catch a good fish by bottom fishing as by spinning/fly fishing.

In general, the returns for sea fishing effort in January, February and March (other than flounder fishing) never lived up to our hopes and, in consequence, we have over the years gradually come to devote January and February to the pursuit of pike, grayling, roach and dace which are abundant in our local rivers. March is now spent fishing for salmon which, although they are by no means abundant at that time of year, are satisfactorily large. Since angling for salmon requires an almost mindless dedication, it makes a relaxing change before sport in the sea begins to pick up again. Had we lived further north or east no doubt the cod would have received our attention in the winter months.

Dinghy fishing is now summarised in a similar manner.

Year	man hours (total)	man hours (per fish)	man hours (per good fish)
1	183	0·5	4·1
2	132	0·9	4·3
3	95	0·6	4·3
4	94	0·8	4·2
Average	126	0·7	4·2

TABLE 8   Bottom fishing from a small rowing dinghy.

The results are better than those of either type of beach fishing whether we consider all fish or just 'good' fish. In fact, since many of the small fish caught for bait were not recorded the 'action' was often considerably more hectic than is suggested by the figures. Also we have excluded mackerel from consideration because a single evening's feathering could distort things considerably.

Our best year's fishing ever included fifty-six 'good' bass and over sixty 'good' mullet. The largest bass weighed 12½lbs and the largest mullet 6¼lbs.

Our best fish of other species from the beach are: conger 40lbs, flounder 3½lbs, pollack 12¼lbs and sole 2½lbs.

From the dinghy we have caught black bream 3½lbs, blonde ray 16lbs, cod 24lbs, conger 46lbs, small-eyed ray 14lbs and a thornback ray of 17lbs.

Other 'good' fish caught were a blonde ray of 24lbs, tope of 40lbs and a turbot of 20lbs.

We are always keen to try out new techniques or to adapt old ones if these will help us to catch more or better fish. There is never any lack of ideas but few of these succeed on the first attempt. If a promising method should fail we reason out why, change it accordingly, and try again. The ideas and methods discussed in this book should be adapted to suit local conditions wherever or however you may fish.

The preferred food of each fish species may vary a good deal according to time and place. The reader will also have noticed that the preferred food of a species and the baits which are used successfully are not always the same thing. The curious preferences of cod for various tastes, the way in which wrasse, which rarely eat fish, may be caught on fish-like plugs and the alacrity with which crustacean-feeding pouting and poor cod will take worm baits are just a few examples. Why should this be? Possible explanations include:

a.   he bait used maybe acceptable but not normally available to the fish.
b.   Tethered baits are easily caught by the fish whereas the genuine, free-living, article, maybe able to escape.
c.   Lures may resemble injured fish. Everyone must have noticed how even placid aquarium fish will attack a crippled member of their community.
d.   It is probable that many more fish would be caught if more attention was paid to fish diets and bait presentation.

In conclusion, in case the reader has not yet realised the full depth of our dedication to angling, in addition to sea fishing we spend annually about 100-200 man hours fishing for salmon (10-20 man-hours per fish) and trout. Also about 200 man hours are devoted to coarse fishing. Last winter however, the coarse fishing was reduced to a minimum because we spent most of our spare time in preparing this book.

We could not, by any stretch of imagination, be regarded as fair weather fishermen (sometimes it is quite the reverse). For example, we have tried to fish Poole Harbour (the Arne Peninsula) for flounders, on a day so cold that 2-ounce leads would not penetrate the surface layer of ice. We have, foolishly, fished from the steep and jagged rocks of Worbarrow Tout in a force eight with huge seas breaking above our heads. Harry, on one occasion, fished a Chesil Beach Christmas Match in which, because of the extreme cold, he was eventually left in sole charge of six rods as his five companions gradually retreated to the warmth and solace of the nearby pub; nothing was caught.

The non-angler will often comment to the effect that fishing is boring, sedentary or an old man's pastime. We can only suggest that such individuals should try spinning or fly fishing from the beach. This may involve a two/or three-mile hike to the sea and hours of continuous walking and casting at a rate of approximately one cast every minute. This means that in three hours spinning the lure will have covered over four miles of water. Finally, there is the inevitable uphill drag back to the car.

Fishing is a time-consuming hobby. According to the National Angling Survey, carried out by the Natural Environment Research Council in 1970, the average sea angler puts in about 180 hours of fishing per year. Most of this time is spent in search of cod, bass and flat fish although bass, it appears, are caught less often than they are sought. The Survey suggests that sea angling is the fastest-growing branch of the sport and at that time there were 1 280 000 sea anglers, over half of whom normally fished inshore or from beaches. We dedicate this book to all our fellow sea anglers and, in particular, to those who have bought it!